The Apprenticeship to Love

The Apprenticeship to Love:
A Field Guide for Finding Love that Works for Life

by R. Phillip Colon, PhD

iUniverse, Inc.
New York   Bloomington

iUniverse books may be ordered through booksellers or by contacting:

iUniverse
1663 Liberty Drive
Bloomington, IN 47403
www.iuniverse.com
1-800-Authors (1-800-288-4677)

ISBN: 978-1-4401-2768-7 (sc)
ISBN: 978-1-4401-2770-0 (hc)
ISBN: 978-1-4401-2769-4 (ebook)

Library of Congress Control Number: 2009925150

Printed in the United States of America

iUniverse rev. date: 06/01/2009

To my wife, Nira, and daughters, Lee and Talia—
the women who have taught me the meaning of love
and rapture.

Contents

Acknowledgments

Writing this book has been an affirmation of the many blessings in my life, which take the form of mentors, loved ones, family, friends, and colleagues. I would like to thank Dr. Arthur Stein, whose teachings are the basis of the Apprenticeship to Love program. Not to be forgotten are my colleagues, friends, and family who helped me formulate my ideas and encouraged me during rough patches of the writing process: Irene Hajisava, Jerry Kleiman, Norman Fried, Jenny Heinz, Ken Kaye, Noelani Colon-Barrister, LuAnn Skolnik, PJ Ehalt, Carmen Colon, and Donald Walton. Many thanks to Michael Malen, who selflessly edited the manuscript, Vered Zehavy for content editing, and Lee Colon, my daughter, who helped provide greater clarity in my writing at a time when I could not see the forest for the trees. Other wonderful members of my family deserving thanks are my wife, Nira, and daughter, Talia, who loved, supported, and encouraged me unwaveringly throughout the whole writing process. Thanks to Orna Lanir, for her talent in helping design the book cover. Finally, there are the thousands of people I have treated in my practice or talked to in the course of giving seminars who taught, encouraged, and inspired me by sharing their life stories.

Preface

This book was conceived and inspired as a result of my mentorship under Arthur Stein, PhD. Dr. Stein is a psychologist, scholar, and visionary in the field of clinical psychology and family therapy.[1] In his seminars, Dr. Stein taught how important the family and family relationships are in the development of health and well-being in all people. He spoke of how the parental relationship is the hub of the family, providing the foundation for the development of all its members emotionally, intellectually, socially, and spiritually. Dr. Stein believed the level of a child's development to be determined by the maturity level of his or her parents. Parents can only teach what they know. Understanding this, Dr. Stein emphasized the importance of increasing an individual's personal competence in relationships and in all aspects of human functioning. After all, better people make better parents, and the road to betterment can be paved by love and marriage. Dr. Stein encouraged single clients to seek out and choose a mate with a high level of ability and potential. He envisioned the creation of a union committed to "a lifetime of getting better one day at a time."[2] Toward this end, Dr. Stein devised The Program of Three, an instructional networking program designed to teach single men and women about love, relationships, and how to find a marital partner while under his care and supervision. I used my mentor's program in my private practice for many years, drawing from

---

1   His teachings were the basis of Diana and Sam Kirschner's book,
Comprehensive Family Therapy (New York: Brunner/Mazel, 1986).
2   Stein, personal communication.

it to develop the methods comprising the Apprenticeship to Love program and eventually this book.

Dr. Stein's program and the methods in this book guide apprentices through a step-by-step process designed to promote growth and positive change. During my time with him, Dr. Stein spoke of his belief that long-term solutions to many of the world's problems, including efforts for world peace, ultimately lie in the health, intactness, centrality, and emotional development of families. He taught his students that healthy love, the core of a good marital relationship, is not a mere feeling, but a profound dynamic process that engenders high-level functioning. Healthy family members could solve problems, large and small, by simply participating in society with the foundation of a loving family. Love, relationships, and family would ultimately save the world. This book addresses the first part of that quest and journey, helping people find each other and develop loving relationships to form healthy families and a better world.

This book was written as a guide that is meant to be read and reread more carefully, as many of the points made are simple truths that can take time to master. Rereading this book as you go through your apprenticeship will provide an enhanced contextual understanding, bringing theory and concepts to life.

Names and details have been altered to protect the identity and privacy of people used in the examples throughout the book.

Introduction
Enduring Love Is Not Easy, Just Worth It

You're in a bind, wanting to find a partner for life, yet feeling stuck due to anxiety or fear. Maybe you don't even know why you're stuck. All you know is that past relationships have not worked out and you haven't been able to find that special somebody. Perhaps you feel ready or would like to be ready. The likelihood is that you have picked up this book because you are a casualty of love. If you are, this book is for you. You want to try again but desire a different, better outcome—one that is enduring and actually happy. If you are looking for a quick solution, don't look here. This book does not offer gimmicks or magical solutions, just a practical approach that works. If you haven't been wounded by love but would like to know how to find a marital partner who is right for you, keep reading. Since this program successfully works for the love challenged, it will work for you.

Your ambivalence about entering the dating scene again gets reinforced by what you see around you. It seems that just about everyone wants a loving partner to be married to for a lifetime, yet divorce statistics show the odds are against this happening. Even worse, of the couples that stay together long-term, few seem to be happy and many would not choose their current partner if given the opportunity to do it over again. Does that mean that seeking a successful marriage is like buying a Lotto ticket, hoping for the best, but expecting otherwise? If that's what you think, you should know that it doesn't have to be that way.

To begin with, don't look around you for answers; it should be obvious by now that most others don't know what they're doing either. Make up your mind that you have to be a pioneer in love, exploring new emotional and relationship territories. The only frightening parts of this process will be your reaction to venturing into new places and painful memories that might resurface when you get nervous. Are you worried that this is more than you are ready for? Don't be. We'll just have to be sure that your efforts take into account your level of readiness, social-skill set, and emotional management ability. It makes sense that to become part of the successful minority you will need to expend energy and learn new skills. That doesn't mean that it is all work and no play. In fact, the process is interesting, fun, and, at times, joyful.

Sound like a lot of work? Anything new and unfamiliar feels that way. Doesn't seem worth it to you? Hopefully, you're still in the bookstore or library and can simply put the book back on the shelf. Any good relationship requires effort, flexibility, open-mindedness, creativity, commitment, and much, much more—in other words, work. But work can be pleasurable and gratifying if it is also meaningful. Your effort can truly be a labor of love, with all the rewards and benefits. Consider the process of learning a part of your preparation and maturation for enduring love, and enjoy yourself along the way.

Why is it that so many people, particularly divorcé(e)s from long-term relationships, dread the prospect of reentering the dating scene? More often than not, it is because they are terrified of feeling inadequate, being rejected, or having another failed relationship. Ironically, the best way to start the Apprenticeship to Love program is to operate on the working premise that you *don't* know enough about people or relationships to have another one at the present time, or any time in the immediate future. This is a great premise as it provides protection from yourself since you are less likely to rush into another relationship. It also provides a great defense from others. For example, you can tell a person who may be trying to rush a relationship that you are not ready for one without having to feel guilty or thinking that you have to "run away." You have been liberated from having to know what you are doing, as you are not expected to be an expert. Now maybe you can relax and have fun meeting new people without having the pressure that comes with expectations. The objective is to learn more about yourself, people, and relationships. Knowledge is power; it lets you identify and avoid unhealthy, dead-end relationships. It also lets you see and know who is a viable love candidate. The Apprenticeship to Love program combines knowledge and practical experience to guide you in meeting, identifying, and engaging the kind of person you can have a good relationship with—somebody who has something to offer you in a relationship, not just the other way around. The very process of searching for this somebody also becomes a pathway for healing and developing the emotional and relationship skills you need to sustain the love you find. Most important, you do it at your own pace and at a level of readiness that is determined by *you*. How? Through *incremental success*—a program that begins at the simplest level to allow you to follow through with set objectives and becomes more complex as you evolve.

Sadly, fun and joy can get lost in hurtful and negative past experiences. Unfamiliar situations can feel potentially dangerous and are, therefore, likely to be avoided. What people often forget are the fun and pleasure that can be found in new experiences. There are three factors that can determine whether you feel able to venture out into the dating scene: physical safety, emotional preparedness, and a strategy that works. Having these fundamental elements in place allows you to develop the confidence to try new experiences because they give you the psychological edge to be able to engage in calculated risk. The principles underlying the Apprenticeship to Love program have been known and used by mental health professionals for over thirty-five years to help individuals develop skills to safely enter and successfully negotiate the singles scene after widowhood, divorce, or the collapse of a long-term love relationship.

Yes, you have a busy schedule with lots of things to do; and this program requires time, energy, and effort. But if you are still reading this after all that has been said, you know that you want more in your life. You understand that finding a companion who loves you, who is willing to commit to the relationship, who wants to be a good friend and lover, and who brings out the best in you will make life extra special. Such a person is rare. Don't settle! That person wants to find you too. This is the kind of cause that you can work for with passion and commitment—and have fun in the process.

Are you ready to become a love apprentice and start your personal journey? Let's begin.

Chapter One
The Apprenticeship to Love: An Overview

You are ready to take your first step in this new journey to finding love that works. Now we have to make sure that you're going to be successful in your efforts. Failure only serves to discourage, while success lays the groundwork for further progress. Make wise, well-thought-out decisions and your actions will lead you toward your ultimate goal of finding a partner for life.

As has been said repeatedly throughout the ages, the hardest part of a journey is getting started. The most challenging part of the Apprenticeship to Love program is overcoming initial reservations. It is natural to fear getting hurt, being embarrassed, feeling shy, or failing, particularly if we have:

- been hurt in the past
- never done something like this before
- can't stand feeling vulnerable or inadequate
- don't think too highly of ourselves in the first place

If you haven't felt like this, you're lucky and it will be that much easier for you. The rest of us will get there, too; it'll just take us a little longer. Just keep reminding yourself, healing involves having new options in life. If there are no new experiences that let you know that you are all right and that there are good possibilities for your future, you can feel stuck, and that can be pretty painful. This is a good enough reason to take the risk of a beginning step. We don't have to let old hurts dictate our present lives or our future. So, how do you get started?

Write down a description of the traits and characteristics you think are important in the person you believe would be best for you.

Maybe it looks more like a wish list, but it's really just a way to help you identify what you are looking for in another person, a way of narrowing the field. As you gain more experience in relationships, you are likely to modify the initial traits you identified, reflecting your greater understanding both of other people and of yourself. Be really honest when you list these traits, and don't think too much about them or how they sound when you read them. This is where you begin to learn something about yourself—it's like taking an inventory of what you value in life and in a mate.

Some past participants with a sense of humor have responded that the candidates they meet just have to be "alive," or "at least mammals." While these criteria leave a lot of latitude in finding candidates, they don't provide much direction in mate selection (and are also rather cynical). Here are some examples of the kinds of information you may want to know:

- Do the candidates have to share your same religious faith or beliefs?
- Is it more important that they be attractive on the outside or the inside?
- How intelligent do they have to be?
- How important is it that they are able to talk about themselves?
- Do they have to share similar interests or just be open to exploring new interests?
- Is it important that they be able to work out misunderstandings with you?

- How honest do they have to be?
- How financially secure do they need to be?
- Do they have to be athletic or into sports?
- How important is being physically attracted to one another?
- Is it important if the candidates want children (or more children)?
- Do they have to share a similar energy level as you?
- How social do they need to be?
- Do they have to like your friends?
- How important is it that they have a sense of humor?
- Does it matter if the candidates are the jealous type?

If you don't have an idea of the kind of person that you are looking for, he or she could be right in front of you and you wouldn't even know it. On the other hand, you may be so exacting in the qualities you demand in another person that it is unlikely that anyone will ever be good enough. In fact, you may not meet your own standards. In this program, what we're looking for is a good match with someone whose traits and values align well with yours. The more compatible the traits and values that you and a candidate share, the better the prospects for a good relationship.

So what's the next step?

Start networking until you find and begin to date three potential love interests ("candidates") simultaneously.

An almost universal reaction is one of disbelief. Don't worry. We're going to start at a level and in a way such that *you can do it*. It's not as difficult or unreasonable as it sounds. I'll tell you how you're going to be able to do it in the following two chapters. For now, let me finish laying out the program for you.

There are four reasons why it is important for you to date *three* candidates at the same time. First, dating just one candidate tends to create over-involvement or over-attachment, making management of the relationship more difficult for you. Second, being involved with two candidates still tends to engender stronger feelings than recommended, with a tendency for over-attachment with one of the two. Third, interacting with three candidates allows you to experience minimal involvement while learning the art of successfully managing interactions within the relationship. The goal is to keep the relationships light, manageable, and safe. Lastly, trying to date more than three candidates is simply too confusing, too draining of time and resources, and tends to dilute the relationships to insignificance.

Let's learn from Jessica's experience:

Jessica was married for twenty years before her divorce. When told to begin looking for opportunities to meet men and socialize with three of them, she immediately felt frightened and intimidated at the prospect, saying, "I don't know how to meet one guy, let alone three!" When she was introduced to Kenny by a mutual friend, Jessica felt great. Kenny was good-looking, well-spoken, liked to have fun, and held a good job. He also had never been married. Jessica thought that would be great, because he would have no baggage for her to deal with. Kenny wanted to become serious at a faster pace than she would have liked, but she told herself, "That's the way things go in this day and age." Besides, she liked what was happening. She felt alive again, experiencing sensations she thought she would never have again. She felt happy and in love, and she shared these feelings with Kenny, who neither went out with her again nor returned her calls.

I'm sure that many women who have been in this kind of situation knew what was coming. Jessica, however, did not. That's the point of the Apprenticeship to Love program. It's getting you to know a lot more about people, relationships, and yourself through your experiences of meeting candidates. Jessica could have saved herself a few emotional lumps if she took the time to find out just who Kenny was as a person before giving herself over to him. She should have followed the next principle of the Apprenticeship to Love program.

Keep the relationship with each of the candidates light and casual, at least during the initial phase of the program.

People tend to become emotionally involved too early in relationships. If emotions get stirred too quickly in a relationship, your ability to objectively assess the characteristics of the other person is likely to get clouded. If you can't trust your judgment because it's impaired, you're likely to get hurt more often, and it will feel as if you can't afford to take a risk because you worry that you'll just set yourself up again. But what if *you* felt in control of the relationship? *Then* you could afford to take the risk, couldn't you? I'm not suggesting that you try to control the candidate, but you can control the number and type of interactions that you have with him or her. For example, limit the frequency of communications to every few days rather than every day. We'll be learning a lot more details about managing the relationship in the next couple of chapters. For now, the point is that learning to manage the level and flow of interactions between you and the candidates allows you greater control of your experience. This will help increase your self-confidence about interacting with potential mates.

Let's visit Jessica again several weeks into the program.

Jessica let her family, friends, and coworkers know that she would like to be introduced to men they thought she might find interesting. She met these men without any expectations, with a personal goal of becoming comfortable in meeting new people and having a good time talking to them. At this point, she had two candidates in her personal program and was on the lookout for a third. Because she knew that she was just practicing the art of "meeting and greeting" and was not overly invested in any of the relationships, she simply took any compliments and advances by men as flattery and enjoyed them.

Candidates must be available for a relationship. They must be neither married nor committed to another person.

How are you supposed to know? You ask outright, up front, *before* you meet the candidate. Ask: "Are you currently married? Are you engaged or living with someone, or do you have a significant other in your life?" If the person tells you he or she is "separated," ask: "Are you legally separated? Do you live separately?" Some people say they are separated when they are no longer sleeping in the same room as their spouse.

If you think it's awkward to ask questions like that of someone you've never met in person, think about how awkward it will be when you find out later on that the other person is married, engaged, or living with somebody. Now *that's* awkward. It's true; someone could lie when you ask. If you do find out later on that the person lied to you about a significant involvement, terminate the relationship immediately. Most people, however, tell the truth when asked directly.

Involve each potential love interest in interactions and conversations that reveal information about him or her.

As I previously stated, the most successful relationships are those where people share common values and interests, so you want to learn what you can about each candidate. The only way to do that is by asking questions during the course of conversations. I'm not suggesting that you find out the person's life story on the first meeting or even shortly thereafter. In fact, it's a good idea *not* to ask probing questions in the first couple of get-togethers, as the candidate may experience them as intrusive. For example, asking a question like, "Why did you and your ex break up?" may evoke defensiveness in the other person. Save those kinds of questions for a time when you have developed more trust with the person and it is clear that you actually take a greater interest in him or her. You want to ask questions that reveal what subjects and activities the candidate takes an interest in, what he or she regards to be important, and how the person regards the things that you are involved in. Remember the list that you made at the beginning of this chapter? Let it be a guide as to the kind of information you are seeking. Take note of how he or she relates to you. Does the candidate look at you when talking? Does he/she seem to be interested in what you have to say? Does the candidate seem cynical or prejudiced when talking about people? What is this person's outlook on life? How does it feel to be in this person's presence? You can find out a lot of information during simple, casual conversations and interactions with the other person.

You want to be having fun on these outings. Enjoy the time out, the company, and the conversation with each of the candidates. Think of it more as entertainment than a chore and you will be in a good mind-set. Try not to have expectations about the other person during these meetings. You are simply there to meet, greet, and have an interesting conversation. You don't have to prove anything to anybody, not to yourself or the other person. Remember, you most likely will have to go through quite a number of people before you find the kind of person that is right for you. Make the journey enjoyable.

Identify each candidate's "positive" and "negative" qualities, strengths, and weaknesses.

By taking inventory, you are evaluating not only the kind of person the candidate is, but how he or she stacks up to the criteria you identified in the exercise. You will be using that information throughout the program. This exercise hones your skill in the art of spotting traits in others. Because you will be talking to and meeting quite a number of people, you want to be able to identify desirable traits and shortcomings as quickly as possible. You will be amazed how quickly you will be able to spot potential candidates for your personal program. It's a great skill to develop, and it will save you unnecessary meetings with people not suitable for you. You are also learning what people have available to offer in a relationship and what they do not.

Rank order your three candidates (first, second, and third) according to preference.

Ask yourself the following questions:

- Why is candidate number one the best of the three? What qualities cause me to put this person ahead of the other two?
- Why is candidate number two in the second spot? Which qualities do I like, and what are my reservations?
- Why is candidate number three in the last spot? What are his or her positive characteristics? Which qualities detract? If this candidate could do something to improve his or her ranking, what would it be?

Now you are not only identifying the traits and attributes of the candidates, but evaluating how important they are to you. Particularly at the beginning of the program, each of the candidates chosen may only have a couple or very few of the traits you identified as important for a long-lasting relationship. It is an opportunity to evaluate the health and viability of those traits that are present, particularly if you have not had the chance to experience them in past relationships and interactions.

Tom complained that his ex-wife, Nancy, was too dependent on him. It seemed as if he always had to make decisions about everything in their life together. He felt burdened by the responsibility. After he divorced, Tom met Claire, who was very independent—so independent, in fact, that she seemed to have little time for him. When they were making plans to meet, Claire told Tom that she didn't like his restaurant suggestion and provided some recommendations of her own. If Tom stated an opinion on a topic, Claire felt quite comfortable in declaring her own, which often did not agree with his. Tom became anxious at the prospect of asking Claire out again. When he didn't call Claire, she called him and asked if anything was wrong, making Tom even more nervous.

Claire could be wonderful for Tom, and he could learn a lot from her about relationships if he knew how to manage his experience with her. Though he wished it, he had never had a relationship with a woman who knew her preferences, felt comfortable in expressing them, and was direct in her relationships. Even though he felt burdened when with Nancy, he felt dominant in the relationship and liked that feeling. He didn't know how to relate to a woman on an equal level. We can safely say that Tom was not ready to have a relationship with Claire. However, his experience with Claire helped Tom to understand the traits of an independent woman and realize that being with such a person required him to be more flexible in his thinking and more comfortable with himself—he didn't always have to be in control. If he couldn't do that, then a relationship with Claire would not be workable and he would need to consider a less assertive woman. Keep in mind that there is no "good" or "bad" in this situation, just what works and what doesn't. It would be wrong for Tom to judge Claire poorly because of his (unacknowledged) insecurities.

By taking inventory of each candidate's attributes, you are also identifying what specifically draws you to a particular person. You are then in the position to know experientially whether the trait you are drawn to works well for you in a relationship.

Doreen liked going out with Frank. He suggested interesting places to go and nice things to do. He seemed like the strong, silent type, which intrigued her even more since it added a dimension of mystery to their meetings. As time went by, Doreen came to realize that she actually knew very little about Frank. After they were dating a while, Doreen began to ask Frank questions about his life experiences and his past. She found that he didn't like to disclose almost anything about himself and changed the topic as soon as he became uncomfortable. Doreen concluded that she was uncomfortable with having no access to Frank's inner life, even though he was a nice guy to do things with. Doreen worried that she wouldn't know when something was wrong or be able to work anything out if there was.

Because Doreen wasn't overly involved with Frank, she was able to enjoy his company and yet see that there was little future in their relationship. She could identify, experience, and take pleasure in what she was attracted to in him, yet not have to suffer in a dead-end relationship.

Continue networking until you find a fourth candidate. This candidate is to replace one of the original three.

When it is clear that none of the three candidates in your program is the love partner you are looking for, it becomes time to resume an active search for a new candidate. This fourth candidate should have at least one positive attribute that is different from the previous candidates you have dated. That way, you have another new experience to explore. It is also preferable that the fourth candidate have at least some of the positive qualities that you previously identified as important to you in a relationship. As you continue to learn about potential partners through your interactions, you come to realize the diversity of available candidates and how each has something different to offer. The more knowledge you have about the possibilities in relationships, the better you become at selecting higher level candidates to relate to. Dead-end relationships become evident sooner, sparing you wear and tear.

Don't settle! Staying with somebody that you don't care about or who is not right for you is neither good nor fair to you or that other person.

After replacing one of the original three candidates with a fourth one, evaluate each of the candidates' positive and negative qualities. Rank order the candidates, justifying each position as you did previously.

Interestingly, when reevaluating the qualities of the two remaining original candidates, you may find yourself rethinking your original perception of each of them, now that you know them better. Maybe you perceived something about one of them but second-guessed yourself, only to have your original observation confirmed. It's possible that you have to trust your instincts more. Maybe you discovered you had overlooked what now seems to be an obvious trait, positive or negative. Was it that well hidden, or were you simply not paying attention? The more time you take to learn about another person, the more you will discover.

Rachel was Josh's number-one candidate, until he met Sara. He liked Rachel's quick-wittedness and sarcastic sense of humor. It was not until Josh met Sara, who also had a good sense of humor, that he realized how judgmental and critical Rachel really was. While still enjoying Rachel's company, Josh realized he was more attracted to what he perceived to be Sara's more positive outlook on people.

It is likely that the positions of the existing candidates will change when introducing a new one into the equation. The candidate that held the number-one position may now be number two or even number three based on the new assessment. Your values and life-guiding principles become most evident when taking inventory and rank ordering the candidates. The traits and characteristics of the candidates that are the deal makers and breakers become most visible here.

Keith met Pat through an Internet dating service for people sharing the same religious faith. He liked that she was a warm, caring, generous person with a good sense of humor. Most of all he enjoyed having a good time with her and partaking in shared interests. They both had children from previous marriages, strong financial obligations, and limited incomes. As Keith began to learn more about Pat, he realized that she was living well beyond her economic means. Though well aware of her mounting debt, Pat continued to buy lavish gifts and expensive clothes and was planning a costly vacation with her children. When Keith tried to gently say something to Pat about her spending practices, she became defensive and told him that he need not be concerned.

While Keith was initially attracted to Pat's many positive personal attributes, he realized that her spending practices and lack of regard for her mounting debt diminished her potential as a life partner for him.

Continue networking and looking for potential candidates to replace any or all of the three currently in your program.

As the journey progresses, the candidates that you choose to include in your program ought to best reflect an increasing level of emotional and relational availability. The more practice you have in selecting candidates and getting to know them, the more you develop an evolving understanding of what qualities make for a better life mate. You come to know what characteristics make for a better, more enduring love relationship. Accordingly, several generations of candidates for each of the three positions are recommended. Each new candidate should have more to offer in a relationship than the person being replaced in your program. Each generation of new candidates becomes an affirmation of your personal evolution and relational savvy.

But what if it's not like that for you? What if you keeping meeting essentially the same person—someone with a different name and body but the same limitations? What happens then? Remember that it's a learning process, which merely means that there is more that you need to know. But rather than simply going by trial and error, you can look for repetitive patterns in your selection of program participants. Don't be afraid to ask yourself some tough questions (or if you are, don't let that stop you). You may not like the answers as to why you are stuck, but the realizations can be both surprising and liberating. For example:

- Are you repeatedly attracted to the same type of person, with unfulfilling results?
- Are you are drawn to the company of candidates who don't respond well to you?
- Do you seem to be more interested in meeting with your chosen candidates than the other way around?
- Do you find more faults than good points in the chosen candidates?
- Do you keep finding yourself to be the third leg of a love triangle whenever you find somebody you really like?

Some of the questions may require straightforward reflection. Others may need the assistance of a good friend or a counselor. Either way, taking measures to get at what's underlying the results allows you to rethink or re-strategize your approach.

Don't be surprised if you conclude that you have hit a ceiling barrier in the level of the candidates available to you. It is likely that your current social and professional circle offers too limited a variety of people to choose from. You may need to branch out to a new social and/or professional circle. (This will be discussed in the next chapter.)

You are not to have sex with any of the candidates. If you do, the candidate involved is to be immediately discharged from the program.

Since candidates are meant to be replaced, they can feel hurt or used when sex has been part of the interaction. Remember, safety is paramount in this program, both for you and anybody you involve as a candidate. Also, it is difficult to maintain the needed objectivity for dating three candidates when your emotions are challenged, and this occurs once sex is introduced into the picture. The relationship with the candidate where sex is involved becomes increasingly difficult to manage. It's not unusual for there to be an increase in the demand of time, attention, and level of involvement by that candidate, because they see the relationship as having been taken to the next stage. One or both individuals can begin to develop emotional feelings for the other that neither of you may be ready for.

Male and female apprentices have commented on the pressure they feel to have sex when dating. Often said is how difficult it can be to decline sex without appearing wimpy, uptight, or generally less than masculine or feminine. While I talk more about that in a short while, just remember that people can and do make unreasonable demands, using guilt ("I thought you liked me") or fear ("I'm not sure if I can continue to see you if you keep holding back from me") as tools to get what they want. If you can't afford to say "no" to sex with another person, you can't afford to say "yes." If somebody is pressuring you to do something you do not want to do, despite the fact that you have told that person that you do not want to do it, then he or she is not demonstrating regard or respect for you. If you are submitting to doing something you really do not want to or feel ready to do, you are not taking good care of yourself. Either way, it makes for an unhealthy situation that you do not want and that you have the power to do something about.

While there are no magic words that will make another person understand and accept your preferences, here are some statements that can make for a clear message:

- "I don't engage in casual sex."
- "I need to know a person well, for at *least* six months, before having sex." (You are testing their level of interest, and you will need to determine your own feelings about this candidate by then.)
- "I'm not ready for sex in our relationship."
- "No."

If the other person continues to insist, simply ask, "Are you trying to pressure me into something I don't want to do?" If the other person says "no" but continues anyway, you have your true answer and it's time to discharge the candidate from the program entirely. On the other hand, if you set a limit and the other person is respectful of your wishes, you have learned something positive about the candidate. It seems hard for some apprentices in this day and age to understand or accept that you do not need to spend a lot of time thinking or worrying about how to set this limit with another person. No means no.

Because Vanessa was out of the dating scene for a long time and felt unsure of herself, she had difficulty setting limits with men around the issue of sex. Shortly after being diagnosed with a gynecological problem that required prolonged treatment and abstinence from sex, she met Dwaine. During the course of their relationship, the topic of sex arose. She explained to Dwaine that she could not have sex because of "doctor's orders" and would not be able to for a period of months. The other two candidates in her program disappeared when they were similarly informed, but, to Vanessa's surprise, Dwaine did not. The unlikelihood of sex removed the topic from consideration entirely, allowing Vanessa and Dwaine to experience other aspects of their relationship, such as sharing good communication, discovering and partaking in common interests, and enjoying each other's company. Ironically, it was Vanessa's medical problem that enabled her to learn that setting a limit about sex doesn't have to mean the end of a relationship.

You, on the other hand, do not need a medical problem to understand that it is legitimate to set a limit.

If you manage the relationships well, the three candidates involved enjoy their participation in the program, or at least have not been harmed. Since candidates usually do not know that they have been in the Apprenticeship to Love program (or out of it), ex-candidates can be a wealth of new friendships and social contacts for you.

When you meet a candidate with whom you would like to become closer and you are certain the candidate is truly available and interested, the other two candidates are discharged from the program.

When this happens, the primary focus is to experience and study the one relationship. There is a deepening of the bond with the one candidate and issues of intimacy are discussed. It is also a time when you get to know the candidate in a larger context, as you will want to meet and experience his or her family and friends and the intricacies of the person's daily life. If this one candidate does not become a long-term love interest or life partner, you simply resume the networking process, looking for three new candidates to involve. By this point, you know how to do it, know that it works, and can get into action much quicker. You continue this process until you find the person you know is right for you and is committed to the relationship. Because of the importance of this stage in the Apprenticeship to Love program, chapter 4 is devoted entirely to this subject.

Are the cautionary statements made here making you nervous? Remember, knowledge is power. You want to know what to do and what not to do so that you are effective in your efforts.

Now that you know how the program works and what needs to happen, it's time to talk about putting it into action. Chapter 2 will teach you how you're going to meet the candidates to involve in your personal Apprenticeship to Love program.

Chapter Review:
The Apprenticeship to Love Program

An Overview of the Program:

- Write down a description of the traits and characteristics you think are important in the person you believe would be best for you.
- Start networking until you find and begin to date three potential love interests ("candidates") simultaneously.
- Keep the relationship with each of the candidates light and casual, at least during the initial phase of the program.
- Candidates must be available for a relationship. They must be neither married nor committed to another person.
- Involve each potential love interest in interactions and conversations that reveal information about him or her.
- Identify each candidate's "positive" and "negative" qualities, strengths, and weaknesses.
- Rank order your three candidates (first, second, and third) according to preference.
- Continue networking until you find a fourth candidate. This candidate is to replace one of the original three.
- After replacing one of the original three candidates with a fourth one, evaluate each of the candidates' positive and negative qualities. Rank order the candidates, justifying each position as you did previously.
- Continue networking and looking for potential candidates to replace any or all of the three currently

in your program.

- You are not to have sex with any of the candidates. If you do, the candidate involved is to be immediately discharged from the program.
- When you meet a candidate with whom you would like to become closer and you are certain the candidate is truly available and interested, the other two candidates are discharged from the program.

Chapter 2
Meeting and Screening Potential Candidates

This is where theory meets reality as you partake in your own personal journey, having fun in the process. All you need is a mind open to meeting new people and a willingness to try new activities. That may sound like a lot for some of you, but even the hardened cynic (or scared person) can be successful when starting at a reasonable place and taking an approach that will allow you to be effective in your personal Apprenticeship to Love program.

Social Networking

Let's talk about the engine that drives the Apprenticeship to Love program, which is social networking, and the fuel that powers it, incremental success. Social networking involves consistently engaging in broad interpersonal activity, a process that allows you to meet new people for your personal program. Every new person that you meet brings potential access to every individual in that person's life, including siblings, friends, coworkers, and extended family, all of whom can introduce you to a candidate for your personal program.

Liz had had enough of Adam, who had strung her along for more than two years. She finally came to terms with the fact that she was in a dead-end relationship after looking at Adam's actions rather than listening to his words. Liz arranged for a gathering of her family and friends and told them that she was ready to move on. They were delighted as they did not favor Adam. Liz asked for their help by requesting that each person in the room commit to introducing her to a potential candidate. A schedule was created detailing which of her family or friends was responsible for an introduction in a given month.

Liz used her knowledge of how her family and friends felt about her and about Adam as a motivator to have them help her with her Apprenticeship to Love program. Liz knew that meeting potential candidates and having the support of her family and friends would enable her to get over Adam. She began the only way she could guarantee getting started successfully, with love from the important people in her life.

Leslie made the mistake of becoming involved with a married coworker in her office. She wanted to end the relationship, realizing there was no future in it, but found it difficult to emotionally separate from the man. Since she was working for a large corporation with several offices in close proximity to where she lived, Leslie looked at the company Web postings for job opportunities in another location. She found a new position in another office that provided professional challenge and advancement, enabling her to put distance between herself and the ex-boyfriend. The new job also enabled Leslie to meet other single professional women that she came to befriend and with whom she socialized. Denise, one such friend, told Leslie about Brett, a supervisor at another office who had recently ended a relationship. Brett was said to be intelligent, fun loving, and available. Denise organized a social gathering involving several people so as to minimize possible awkwardness in the introduction. Leslie and Brett took an immediate liking to one another. Brett later called Leslie for a date.

By moving to another office, Leslie created access to an entirely new social circle in which to relate, both personally and professionally, in the process making it easier to get over her ex-boyfriend. The anticipated risk involved in the change was offset by the potential of many benefits. Leslie became exposed to the hobbies, interests, and social activities of those she met, providing for novel experiences and additional opportunities for fun. When Leslie met with Denise's friends, she gained access to their families and social circles.

Social networking works, but only if you're doing it. Liz and Leslie are different from one another. Leslie has greater self-confidence, yet both were able to be successful in their efforts. They had different strategies based on their personalities and ability level. Even though some may think Leslie's strategy gutsier than Liz's, one way is no better than the other, and both can be effective. The key here is *incremental success*. It means breaking down a skill, activity, effort, or desired goal into fundamental components that will allow you mastery and effectiveness through your efforts. Despite conventional wisdom, if you make repeated attempts and do not succeed, don't try harder, try something different. Keep scaling back what you are doing or the way you are doing it until you have guaranteed mastery at that level. Once you are confident of your ability at that level, increase the degree of complexity just enough so that you can still be successful some of the time and be sure of mastery with consistent effort. It is crucial to start in a way that guarantees success in your efforts so as to avoid becoming unduly frustrated and discouraged.

Sam was tired of feeling lonely. He had come to terms with the reality of his divorce but felt terrified of reentering the singles scene. Sam decided that it was time to end the drought and meet women. He called a divorced male friend he knew and asked where he could meet single women. His friend, wanting to impress, took Sam to a social club repeatedly advertised on the radio. When they entered the club, Sam was overwhelmed by the lights, music, and what he perceived to be scary-looking women dressed like they were doing a meat market ad. The idea of even approaching one of them was intimidating. By the end of the night, Sam was more discouraged than before.

Besides the fact that dance clubs and bars are terrible places to try to meet potential candidates for this program (though they may be fine to go to with friends to socialize), Sam was simply not ready for this kind of setting, and the experience simply served to confirm his worst fears.

Sam decided he wasn't ready to date, but he was ready to meet new people and have fun. He enrolled in an adult education volleyball class. Sam figured that even if he didn't meet anybody, at least he would be getting out, getting in shape, and having a good time. While at volleyball, he met Donald, another divorcé. They traded divorce war stories, and Sam soon found another person he could relate to and with whom he could socialize. During a holiday party at Donald's apartment, Sam met Annie, a married neighbor. Annie liked Sam so much that she introduced him to her good friend, Cathy, who was also divorced.

By reassessing his situation, Sam changed his course of action, finding something he could do that was a step in the right direction. By participating in new recreational activity and simply being friendly, he allowed new people to come into his life who enriched his experience. It also gave him access to their social circle and new opportunities.

Pardon the chorus, but social networking works. You never know whom you will meet or when or where, but you have to be "out there" in the social world for it to happen. Find an activity that is fun, interesting, meaningful, or whatever will allow you to venture out and meet new people.

Where to Start

Where is the best place to start your personal Apprenticeship to Love program? Right where you are, with the people immediately available to you. Just like something in plain sight can seem hidden because we don't see it, there may already be potential candidates for your program right in front of you. You simply may not have looked at them in that way because they were already there long before you became available. Look again. You may be surprised at whom you see. Broaden the characteristics of the kind of person that you would be willing to date. Try not to limit yourself by size, shape, or other physical limitations that you might otherwise use to reject a potential candidate. As part of your apprenticeship, go out with as many kinds of people as you can, including those you would have disregarded in the past. Go beyond looks or appearances and discover how much more there is to a person. See what there is to enjoy in each person that you meet.

Like Liz, tell your family and friends that you are ready to start meeting new people they think are fun and interesting, not just love interests; tell them to either introduce you if they know of someone, or be on the lookout on your behalf. Your family and friends may be waiting for you to let them know that you are ready. It doesn't matter if the people they are going to introduce you to aren't right for you. This is just the beginning, and it is practice. Besides, the candidates are all meant to be replaced anyway (at least in the beginning), so it matters less where you start than where you finish. In fact, remind yourself that whoever you meet isn't going to be the right person and not to have any expectations other than wanting to spend time in a pleasant manner. You can afford to take this kind of risk, right?

What if the answer is *no*? Then start at a place and in a way in which you feel you can take a chance. For example, start confidence building just by talking to people around you, men and women, wherever you are. That's right, at the office, in line at the store, and while you're sitting in a conference room waiting for a meeting to start. Get used to making casual contact and small talk with people, even with those you have little interest in or no desire to date. There are no expectations (by you), and whatever the outcome, it doesn't have to have significant meaning. It makes the time pass, and you'd be surprised just how easy it is. Most people wait for someone else to start a conversation. If the conversation stops, you just simply go back to whatever you were doing. I am not advising you to pick people off the street. Rather, you are encouraged to get used to having light conversations with people you happen to be with because of circumstances. You may feel shy at first, but you will soon be encouraged by how receptive so many people are. Developing the skill of proactive "chitchat" puts other people at ease as it opens a dialogue.

Incremental Success

Still sounds like too much to be able to do? Using the concept of incremental success, you keep rethinking and re-strategizing your efforts until you find a way to be able to proceed toward your goal. In this case, the goal is meeting new people and becoming more comfortable in social interactions with them. It is possible that you may need to begin with less direct social interactions. For example, visit chat rooms on the Internet and get used to dialoguing online. Go to a chat room in a subject area you take an interest in and have something to say, like a site based on a hobby, a sport, or religious orientation. Start by "listening in" on the conversation and get used to the shorthand and lingo. You'll pick up the shorthand language after a short while. This is not an exercise to meet candidates for your Apprenticeship to Love program, although it is possible. It is meant as an exercise to get you used to making contact with new people and conversing with them. As you become comfortable with this medium, take the opportunity to speak on the telephone to people you meet and get to know, developing your communication skills. When you are ready, you can join an online dating service and begin interactions with the idea of meeting potential candidates.

Remember to keep it simple, looking for similar interests and enjoyable conversation.

Caution: A number of people view the Internet as a source of entertainment and misrepresent themselves, giving information that is not true about their age, marital status, and even gender. While we'll be discussing later some safeguards to always put into place regarding anybody that you don't know, just be reminded here to take your time in getting to know another person or in drawing conclusions about that person.

Can you see how incremental success can work for you? Every time you feel that you have reached an impasse ask, "If I can't do this because it's too hard (or I'm too nervous), then what can I do that's easier and will help me in my efforts?" It doesn't matter where you are in the Apprenticeship to Love program when you feel stuck; applying the principles underlying incremental success will get you "unstuck." It is a great feeling to overcome personal barriers and the victories will boost your self-confidence. Where I see apprentices defeat themselves is when they refuse to concede that they are, in fact, at an impasse or think that there is something wrong in having to simplify their efforts. Pride or self-blame gets in the way of creative problem solving. Learning to work with our vulnerabilities and limitations is key to having a successful life and to being effective in the Apprenticeship to Love program.

Being Socially Available

In order to network socially, you have to be receptive to meeting others. *How socially available are you?* The answer to this question may be a surprise, as some of you may not be as socially available as you think for the purposes of the Apprenticeship to Love program. Mature adults have many responsibilities and very little available time. Colleagues, family, and a small circle of friends usually take up available time and it can even be a challenge to maintain these relationships. The result is that your lifestyle may not readily allow for new people to enter your social circle.

Jane is an extreme example. She said, "I don't have a life of my own. I'm so busy helping my daughter and grandchildren that the only way I'll meet a guy is if I accidentally run him down while driving my grandchildren around."

It's easy to see how Jane had a difficult time meeting anybody new, never mind potential candidates. She did not realize that she had closed her social circle. Jane acknowledged feeling terrified at the prospect of being in another relationship with a man. Being locked into her daughter's life was a way of protecting herself while feeling great love and emotional connection.

Another apprentice, Peggy, had a closed social circle that was harder to see. Even though she was intelligent, attractive, active, and fun, with many friends outside of her family, she had not gone out on a date for more than ten years despite a stated willingness and desire to do so. She simply had depleted her referral sources for potential candidates. While taking inventory of her social network, Peggy realized that she was part of a loving support system made up of fabulous ladies who had all unknowingly given up on meeting men. Peggy concluded that she would be unlikely to enter a love relationship with a man the way her life was organized and decided to consciously expand her social circle. Her working premise was that her true friends would respect and support her efforts.

Expanding Your Social Circle

If not here, somewhere in the process of your personal Apprenticeship to Love program, you will likely conclude that your social circle is too limited for finding candidates and you will need to expand it. Your family and friends may have run out of people for you to meet and you mostly keep meeting the same people in your daily activities. It's time to find new venues to meet people. While "high tech" is easier, the best tried-and-true method of meeting candidates is still through "low-tech" personal introductions, as in being "fixed up." Either way, there is something that everybody can do within their comfort level to socialize and meet new people. It is important that you take advantage of social opportunities that come your way.

Michael met Irene at a social gathering. He enjoyed their conversation, the way they interacted, and how comfortable he felt with her. While talking, Michael discovered that Irene was already involved in a relationship. He asked Irene if she had any friends like her to whom she could introduce him, and he gave her three of his business cards for that purpose.

The likelihood is that Irene does have friends similar to her who would appreciate an introduction to a man "checked out" by a friend and determined to be worthy of introduction.

Sally met Joe at a party. While there was synergy between them and they had many things in common, Joe was married. Sally told Joe what a great time she had had talking to him and told him that she would love to meet any available men he knew who were of his caliber.

Sally is using the connection she feels with Joe to ask him to introduce her to someone he knows is available. She could have even asked to meet Joe's wife at the party, another entry point to a new social circle.

Michael and Sally are working the program. Each is advocating for him- or herself to a person resembling the desired kind of candidate. Since "birds of a feather flock together," there is a good chance that Irene or Joe has similar friends. If someone knows the kind of person you are looking for, he or she will more likely think of you when meeting such a person. The more people thinking of you in such a situation, the more likely you are to find good candidates.

Whenever Gary goes to a business conference in a major city and there is entertainment near the site of the meetings, he buys two tickets to a concert or a show. He then looks for someone in the conference to accompany him. Gary searches for a person he feels comfortable with and finds entertaining. His evenings usually end up quite pleasant at these conferences. Gary has made numerous new business contacts and his network has flourished.

Gary is being proactive in enjoying his time at conferences and is socially open, which has paid off in multiple ways. He looks for someone, man or woman, who is also looking for entertainment and to be social. He knows that the majority of people wait for someone else to initiate good ideas. Being introduced to potential candidates was a byproduct of Gary being positive in thinking and efforts, which draws people to him like a magnet.

Geraldine is widowed and took over her husband's small business after he unexpectedly passed away. She was involved in the business long enough to be able to maintain the company's customer base, giving her time to recover. She spent many hours at the job, meeting with customers but having little time to socialize. After some years, Geraldine wanted to grow the business and decided to join a business networking group. She was the only woman in the group. There, she met Robert, who worked in another industry and who was divorced. They became friendly over a period of months, and then Robert asked Geraldine on a date.

Geraldine did not join the networking group to meet men or to date. Both Geraldine and Robert owned businesses, and they had much in common, including not having much time to get out socially. Their business pursuits and similar lifestyles were a source of attraction for both.

Places to Meet Candidates

One of the most common questions asked of the Apprenticeship to Love program is, "When and where is the best place to meet prospective candidates?" The answer is "anywhere" and oftentimes when you least expect it. However, you increase the chances when you are involved in activities that place you in the company of people with whom you are unfamiliar. Become involved in activities where there is a shared interest by those in attendance. Some examples are: clubs, organizations, lectures, charity events, social events at a neighboring place of worship, adult education classes, and volunteer work. You might also try involving yourself in projects at work with people from other departments or offices, as well as any other activity you find interesting or might enjoy. The list is endless because all that is required is the opportunity to meet new people to interact with. Don't look for the right place to go to or the right activity. Despite what others might tell you, there is no such place or activity. You are looking for any nondestructive venue that places you in a new social context because then you are in a position for social networking. One thing is for sure, if you are home, isolated, bored, and feeling sorry for yourself, you are not in a position to meet candidates. You need to venture out into the world like you belong in it and become involved in new, enjoyable, interesting experiences that make you feel good. The more you enjoy where you are and what you are doing, the more attractive you will feel and be to others, increasing the likelihood of making a connection and entering the network of friends and family of those that you meet.

What to Look For

The second most frequently asked question is what to look for in a preferred candidate. One part of the answer involves knowing what you want and what you don't want. The other part is distinguishing between what you want and what you need in a relationship. The better your developed ability to make the distinction of both preference and need, the easier it will be for you to narrow the field of contenders and identify your future marital partner.

What you *want* in a life partner is fairly subjective and can be thought of as preference. It can be quite changeable and influenced by life experiences, including what you learned in your family, what was thought to be important in your milieu of friends, and a reaction to previous relationships.

For the longest time, Jeff, who is very athletic, was bothered by his wife's disinterest in sports. He thought of her indifference to sports as a wedge in their relationship as he frequently liked to play sports and attend athletic events. Jeff often encouraged his wife to "seek out a passion" of her own. She finally did, finding passion in the game of tennis, where she met another man and divorced Jeff. In retrospect, Jeff realized he had never tried to involve himself in his wife's interests; he had only tried to involve her in his. Now he looks for a woman who likes to be active in her leisure time and is interested in sharing activities with him.

It is important to observe your changing reactions to desired traits in candidates, analyzing if the qualities you found attractive are in fact positive attributes to your relationship or balms for previous painful experiences. Jeff realized that he has to value the interests of the woman he is with if he wants her to value his. Because of the centrality of athletics in his thinking and experience, Jeff confused the level of importance it should have in his relationship. Having a partner who supports your interests is not the same as requiring the person to feel the same way you do about a specific interest. A want can feel like a need, especially if something has been lacking in past experiences. In addition, a want can often lead you to recognize a need that has broader implications for your relationships.

Fariha believed her ex-husband to be "a cold fish" who was never affectionate. Then she met Autri, who showered her with endless attention and seemed to always want to be holding her. Fariha thought she had found her soul mate. After a while, however, she began to feel claustrophobic in the relationship. When she wanted to meet with her girlfriends alone, Autri pouted and Fariha felt guilty. Whenever they were out in public, Autri seemed to be attached to her side.

Having spent years longing for attention and affection, Fariha was drawn to Autri like a hiker parched from a walk in the desert would be drawn to water. Once her longing was satisfied, however, she found Autri's demeanor too overwhelming and restrictive. In this case, Fariha was able to identify her want as a reaction to a previous relationship and to change her priorities for the future. She learned that finding someone that is affectionate and demonstrative is important to her, but needed someone who could also tolerate separateness.

Compatibility of Values and Interests

What you want to look for is compatibility of values and interests between you and the candidates that you meet. The more you and the potential candidate have in common in terms of values and interests, the better. Be real. If you are looking for a person who has everything you do not or is all the things that you think you are not or if you hold that person to a standard that you don't follow, the results are not usually good. However, the concept of becoming involved with someone who has desirable traits or characteristics more evolved than your own can be a good thing.

Marshall was never very good at expressing his thoughts or feelings. Then he met Penny, who was. As happens between almost any two human beings if they are together long enough, misunderstandings arose. Whenever Penny talked to Marshall about a matter that came up, his tendency was to become initially defensive. Marshall felt ineffectual in expressing himself and didn't like the experience. Penny was patient. Instead of simply reacting to Marshall's defensiveness, she reminded him of her intent, which was trying to resolve the matter at hand. She was reassuring and encouraged Marshall to talk about his thoughts and feelings. Between Marshall making efforts to find words to fit his thoughts and experience and Penny asking questions to help clarify his statements, they were able to have productive dialogue. Marshall was surprised and pleased that he could talk in a way he never was able to before and was appreciative of Penny's patience and efforts. He felt more effective and came to take more risks in the things he would talk about and say when with Penny, feeling closer to her in the process.

Workability of a Relationship

Penny was not trying to save or change Marshall. She simply wanted to have a constructive dialogue with someone she liked because that was what she would have tried to do with anyone. Marshall acknowledged his personal deficiency and took the opportunity to see if he could do anything about it, with positive results. Marshall and Penny are both "winners" in this situation. Penny has a better relationship with someone she likes, and Marshall feels better about himself and Penny. This example highlights the importance of "workability" in a relationship. *Workability* refers to the existence of a sufficient level of investment by those involved to develop and maintain the health and viability of the relationship through a commitment to building skills in resolving differences. This commitment is fundamental in ensuring emotional and personal growth in each of the relational members, as it forces new perspectives to be considered, understood, and integrated into the relationship. When searching for candidates, you want to find those who either have good relationship skills or, like Marshall, are responsive to developing them. Remember, you don't need perfection in a relationship, just workability. On the other hand, don't enter a relationship thinking that you're going to change the other person.

Anita liked being with Eric because he was a lot of fun. She had married and later divorced a man she described as cheap, humorless, and asocial. Eric was different. He had lots of male friends and liked going out frequently with "the boys." He spent his money freely on recreational activity and buying Anita expensive gifts. Eric had a rather coarse sense of humor that Anita didn't like, and he gambled too much, but she was drawn to his unconventional style. She also figured that once they were in a relationship, Eric would change his ways. After dating a while, Anita began to chide Eric about his coarse humor, extravagant spending, and frequent gambling, leading to arguments between them. Eric repeatedly told Anita to stop trying to change him. He didn't want to discuss her complaints and favored saying to her, "What you see is what you get!" Anita told herself Eric just needed more time, but he would eventually come around.

It should be clear that this is a dysfunctional relationship in need of termination. If they stayed together, Anita would be perpetually displeased and judgmental of Eric; Eric would be in the position of the proverbial "bad boy." Eric had grown up in a "rough neighborhood" and Anita in a middle-class family. If Eric had an interest in polishing his image and lifestyle now that he had a good job and lived in a middle-class neighborhood, Anita's comments might have been welcomed and appreciated, making the interchanges more productive. More often than not, it is best if you perceive the potential life mate as being good enough "as is" and not as a "fixer-upper." Nobody likes to be perceived or feel like he or she is "run down" and in need of repair.

Tolerance

In considering desirable traits to be on the lookout for, think of *tolerance*, which involves a person's open-mindedness and ability to accept how different you two are from one another. It implies regard and respect for how dissimilar you may be in temperament, outlook, energy level, or approach to life. The more tolerance present, the greater the amount of diversity the relationship can handle.

Forgiveness

Another desirable, if not fundamental, trait to seek out in a relationship is that of the *capacity for forgiveness*. It is painful to be with somebody who holds grudges or who can't seem to get beyond the pain of what has happened. Living with a person who blames you for mistakes that have long passed and perpetually holds you responsible for his or her suffering is miserable. Forgiveness is essential for healing well from painful experiences in any relationship.

The Three Cs of a Successful Relationship

The three Cs of any successful, long-term, loving relationship that you should be looking for are: *Communication, Caring,* and *Commitment.* Being able to communicate with a love partner is very important. It is what allows you to plan, clarify, collaborate, resolve differences, express feelings, let perspective be known, and much, much more. It is true that there are many people who *do* rather than *say* and that actions are more important than words, but being able to speak to each other with candor and directness can make the relationship a whole lot easier and more satisfying.

Caring is another cornerstone of a loving relationship. It is the positive regard that you feel for the one you love and vice versa, and it underlies intimacy and affection. The sense of caring fuels compassion and thoughtfulness between people. It also inspires self-restraint when one is hurt and angry so as not to take it out on the loved one, even if the other person is thought to be responsible.

Finally, commitment is the glue that keeps the relationship together when things have deteriorated, until you and your life partner can find a way to make things right again. Look for these important traits in your candidates, and see if they evolve as your relationship does.

Healthy Investments

Fundamental in all of the traits previously mentioned is an investment in health (physical/emotional/relational), well-being, and healing. These investments can define priorities as well as perspective and guide actions both in and out of a relationship. For example, they can help define what the right thing would be in tending to a difficult situation. Since there are few self-actualized people walking around (not counting those who *think* they are), it is best to seek out others who are open to and want to be better people in the context of a relationship. You and your love mate can spend a lifetime together enjoying each other's company, looking for fun opportunities, seeking chances to personally develop, and learning to heal from life's unfortunate experiences with the help of one another. That can truly be called "success."

What You Don't Want

Like the saying, "a chain is only as strong as its weakest link," a relationship can only be as happy or healthy as its partners' least capacity to deal with problems. Toward that end, equally as important as what you want in a relationship is what you *don't* want. As a psychologist for many years, I have witnessed the psychological carnage that can be inflicted by one person on another. Trust me. If you can avoid another person with the following traits, please do. High on your list of "don't want" should be the trait of destructiveness (physical or psychological), either towards him- or herself or others (including you). A person who repeatedly engages in hurtful, damaging, or destructive behavior is demonstrating a component to his or her personality. That means, despite what is said by that person, what you are witnessing is not simply situational but rather a pattern of behavior. Expect to see a lot of it if you happen to choose to be with that person. Even if the behavior is toward another person, it's just a matter of time before he or she will be that way with you. Look at what a person does, not only what he or she says. That includes repeated apologies without behavior change.

Another better-to-avoid type of person is one who is extremely self-absorbed, as if people and life revolve (or should revolve) around him or her. ("Enough about me. Let's talk about what you think about me.") This is not to be confused with a secure, assured person, though some initially confuse the difference between the two. The problem with this trait is that there is little room for you being you or you having needs. Emotional needs are reserved mainly for that person, not you. Forget about trying to address something the other person is doing that hurts you as it is experienced as an emotional attack on him or her. Life is happy and good as long as it is defined by that other person and you don't disagree. Anybody who has "been there and done that" with this kind of person will advise you to keep your distance.

Likewise, people who blame and are suspicious of others (it's always somebody else's fault) or are emotionally unpredictable (it feels like you're walking on eggshells around them, always afraid to set them off) can wear you down to nothing over the course of time.

Frankly, *everybody* has problems. In fact, someone who believes that he or she doesn't have *any* has even bigger problems. What makes the aforementioned traits in another person so undesirable (please lose that person's number) is how unlikely the other person is to change for the better; as a result of this inflexibility, the situation becomes "unworkable." You want somebody who is willing to acknowledge problems as they arise and is committed to self-improvement (verified by changed behavior). That way, you both can improve together while striving to have a good life.

Finding a Coach

Are you nervous that you may not be able to distinguish between candidates you want versus those you want to avoid? Working closely with a coach on your Apprenticeship to Love program can help. A coach can be a family member or a friend. It can be most anybody that you trust, who has your welfare and well-being foremost in their thinking when discussing these matters and whose judgment you regard and respect. Your coach must be a person who can be direct and is willing and able to say things about you or the person(s) you are seeing that may be difficult to hear. If there is nobody like this in your life, consult with a licensed mental health professional who would be willing to act as your coach. The role of the coach is to objectively review the candidates or potential candidates with you. He or she acts as your extra eyes and ears to help evaluate the candidates more effectively and appraise your progress. A coach can keep you on track in your efforts and be supportive when you're feeling weak, uncertain, or vulnerable. You want to be able to talk about what seems to get in the way. Look for a coach (or even a second coach) who can creatively brainstorm with you on how to gain entry into new social circles. Choose carefully as what he or she says is likely to affect the course of your efforts and influence your perspective.

Obstacles

Two obstacles frequently cited by divorced apprentices in their efforts to find potential candidates are a lack of time and a lack of opportunity, because of work or child rearing. There is a vast difference in available time and opportunity between a working custodial parent of two children with little to no family support and a person with adult sons or daughters or no children in the household. However, the distinction between the two situations mainly involves different considerations and kinds of creativity rather than feasibility. For example:

Rosemary is divorced and has custody of her two children, both under ten years old. She says her ex-husband is irresponsible and rarely sees the children, giving Rosemary little free time. Rosemary works and pays for day care, leaving very little extra money. Undeterred, she sought out the company of other single working mothers, forming a social and support group. The group of friends organized a rotating babysitting schedule, taking turns watching the children while the others socialized together, completed necessary errands, or went out on dates.

Rosemary has a healthy attitude about her circumstances. She is determined to have as full a life as her situation will allow. She also has a great group of coaches available at her disposal. You can see how her creativity and resourcefulness can be applied in meeting potential candidates. You can either think of Rosemary as someone special in her approach or understand that she is just trying to live her life well, which is exactly what you want to be doing.

Program Safety

There are certain things that need to be said in the name of safety, even at the risk of raising your anxiety. Actually, if you follow these simple rules, you have less to worry about. Here are some common-sense precautions that you should take whenever and wherever you meet a new person in order to keep yourself safe and in control of the situation.

- Don't rush or be rushed. Take the opportunity to learn more about the other person, over the course of time, without becoming overly involved.
- If you meet someone at a club or a party, don't leave with that person alone. Set up another meeting time at a place of your choosing.
- Do not take anybody you meet through a computer very seriously or at face value. Many view the Web as a recreational outlet or source of entertainment. The person on the other side of the computer screen may be a different age, gender, or marital status than stated; and many of the facts given could be suspect.
- Do not give a stranger your home address or meet someone you don't know (or know little about) at your residence. Choose a public place to meet with ready access to transportation and get yourself there.
- Give your cellular or business telephone number rather than your home number at the beginning.
- Let someone know where you're going and who you're with.

Try not to get alarmed or discouraged by these words of caution, as they are simply reminders that it takes time to know who the other person really is. A frequently favored way of having a first contact is via the telephone. It is an emotionally safe medium that allows you to hear what the person is like at a time and place of your choosing. You can ask questions and get information about the potential candidate, making it a good screening device that spares you unnecessary meetings. An ideal place to have a first meeting is a place where you are investing very little time and money, like a coffee shop. The less invested you are in the person or the situation, the better. Be more invested in the process of networking. A mistake frequently made by apprentices is investing too much time or money in meeting a new candidate, creating higher expectations and greater disappointments. It is better to think of the process as a hobby or a sport that you take an interest in and are trying to learn. If you are not enjoying the process, you may need to rethink your expectations or how you are going about it.

If you can meet one candidate for your Apprenticeship to Love program, you can meet more. It's a matter of continuing your social networking, which becomes easier with time and can be very entertaining. The goal of juggling three candidates in your life, however, is very challenging. There are, after all, so many hours in a day and you have other responsibilities. The next chapter will address how to manage relationships with three candidates.

Chapter Review:
Meeting and Screening Potential Candidates

Social Networking involves consistently engaging in broad interpersonal activity, a process that allows you to meet new people for your personal program. Every new person that you meet brings potential access to every individual in that person's life, including siblings, friends, coworkers, and extended family, all of whom can introduce you to a candidate for your personal program.

Incremental Success involves thinking and strategizing your efforts in a way that guarantees attaining your goals. Break down your actions to the simplest level that will guarantee that you can start and complete your efforts. Each success encourages you to make a new effort towards your incrementally higher level goals.

Points to Consider:

- Evaluate how socially available you really are.
- Expand your social circle to increase the likelihood of meeting new people.
- Become involved in activities where there is a shared interest by those in attendance.
- What you want in a relationship may not be the same as what you need.
- Look for compatibility of values and interests between you and the candidates that you meet. The more you and the potential candidate have in common in terms of values and interests, the better.
- When searching for candidates, you want to find those who either have good relationship skills or are responsive to developing them.

- A good trait to look for in a candidate is that of *tolerance*, which involves a person's open-mindedness and ability to accept how different you two are from one another.
- Another desirable trait to seek out in a relationship is the *capacity for forgiveness*.
- The three Cs of any successful, long-term, loving relationship are: *Communication, Caring,* and *Commitment*.
- Find someone to be your coach. This person must be direct and willing to say things about you or the person(s) you are seeing that may be difficult to hear.
- Use common-sense precautions whenever you meet a new person in order to keep yourself safe and in control of the situation, e.g. never give a stranger your home address and choose a public place to meet.

Chapter Three
The Art of Prospecting for Love with Three Candidates

Now that you have learned how to identify and get candidates to participate in your personal Apprenticeship to Love program, it is time to get skilled at managing your three relationships and learning what you can from each one of them. This particular phase of the program is the most significant and rewarding. You will learn the most about yourself and the people to whom you are attracted, and you will master identifying the kind of relationship that best suits you.

First, let's talk about some of the actual ways to manage several relationships. Some of the points were touched on in chapter 2, but we will expand upon them here.

Form a Controllable Level of Involvement with Each of the Candidates

Having a sense of control over the pace of the relationship allows you to feel emotionally safe enough to risk participation. You are able to feel emotional security by managing your feelings well in relation to the other person. Maintaining a level of objectivity about your feelings and in your assessment of the candidate increases the likelihood of personal effectiveness when drawing conclusions and making decisions during the program. If you are in over your head, it can be an emotional rollercoaster. Unmanageable feelings cloud the capacity to see and read information correctly, which can lead to mistakes and heartache. However, you also do not want to be too emotionally distant from your candidate, or you will not feel a connection to that person.

There are several factors that can challenge your ability to control the pace of the relationship: loneliness, sexual frustration, desire for companionship, need for affection, yearning to be loved, or pressure from family members, to name a few. Pressure coming from outside, like from friends and family, can be easier to deal with than emotional pressure from within. For example, a female apprentice had noted that while blessed with friendships, she had not dated for over ten years. Human needs are real and can be experienced strongly. Pushing for a relationship out of need, without reconciling who the other person is and his or her appropriateness for you, is likely to produce unfortunate results. Internal emotional pressure can make you move faster than you want to and in ways that are difficult to control, especially when you don't realize what is driving the feeling. That is why you need to carefully monitor and manage the experience from the onset. For example, ask yourself, "Do I look forward to seeing this particular candidate because of how much I like being with him or her, or is it because I don't want to be home alone on Saturday night?" Either answer is okay, as long as you are fairly clear as to what your feelings are.

The fact is that the phenomenon of attraction can be quite complex to understand. For example, were you ever attracted to another person because he or she had beautiful eyes or hair, nice hands, or a nice smile? Most people have been. Likewise, we can be drawn to a calm demeanor, a good sense of humor, self-confidence, or a fun-loving personality. Many traits and characteristics comprise the human persona, and the consistent display of certain qualities shapes how an individual is perceived by others. When considering a candidate, it is possible to be attracted to a narrow component of the candidate's personality, rather than the whole. For example, we can be drawn to a trait or characteristic in a candidate that we think is absent in ourselves or in our previous relationships. Suddenly having a long-desired experience can be both intoxicating and terrifying, which makes managing the relationship difficult. The tendency is to either become over-involved too quickly or to become so anxious that you have the impulse to run away.

David's relationship history was a portfolio of being drawn to physically attractive women whom he would later conclude to be "unintelligent and needy." While he liked feeling superior to these women, who often flattered him, David talked about wanting a relationship with an attractive, intelligent, successful, independent, professional woman worthy of being a "life partner." When he met Karen at a party, he thought he had met the woman of his dreams and felt enamored of her. He started to call Karen frequently, like he had the other women, but Karen said he was "coming on too strong." David professed his deep feelings to Karen fairly quickly, but she asked how he could feel that way when he didn't know her. David began to feel very insecure, not knowing how to act toward Karen and what to do about his feelings. He came to the conclusion that Karen was "cold" and began to avoid her. Calling one of the women with whom he felt safe made him feel better.

David didn't realize that the women he surrounded himself with were a distorted reflection of how he felt about himself. He hated feeling "needy" and therefore disliked that trait when he saw it in the women he dated, even as he exploited the trait to get closer to them. David had low self-esteem, so he judged women as inferior in order to feel better about himself. As a result, he couldn't allow himself to see a fuller, more realistic view of the women he dated; instead, he related to a narrow (distorted) version of them created by his own insecurities. When David met Karen, the woman he idealized, who was comfortable with herself, direct, and an effective communicator, he was unprepared to relate to her in a mature way. We can see how David was in way over his head, guided by his emotional states, while Karen was not. Karen kept a manageable emotional distance that maintained her objectivity, enabling her to deal with David effectively and spare herself grief.

It is important that you take the time to learn the whole of the people you date—the sum of the different personality traits and characteristics of each person. As a learning exercise, I encourage you to seek out, identify, and explore the various candidates' identities from a safe, manageable distance. Of course, as it is no easy task, I will elaborate on how you can create and maintain this ideal emotional stance.

Maintain Infrequent Contact with Each Candidate, Speaking Every Few Days at the Most

In this day and age of answering machines, voice mail, cell phones, the Internet, Blackberries, text messaging, "tweeting," and various other devices and forms of communication, it can be a real challenge to manage the frequency of contact with others. If someone can't contact you one way, they can try in other ways and reach you at work, in the supermarket, at a restaurant, walking down the street, driving, and even in the bathroom. The good news is that most communication devices have features that allow contacts to be screened. In general, it is best if *all* forms of contact, including non-face-to-face contact with candidates be kept to a minimum. You can understand how the frequency can escalate quickly given the many available options. *Remember, it is easier to limit the number of contacts from the onset than to try to reduce them later on.*

If used skillfully, the many non-face-to-face forms of contact are actually a real asset in the Apprenticeship to Love program. They allow for interaction and dialogue from an emotional and physical distance and give you the ability to discontinue the contact immediately, if wanted, with minimal effort or discomfort. Best of all, you can decide whether or not to have contact at all. Remember, you are not obligated to return an e-mail, phone call, or any form of communication immediately. If a candidate asks why you haven't returned his or her messages, simply state that you have been busy, otherwise involved, don't check your messages often, got home too late, or were simply too tired. Or you can simply state that you like to take things very slowly in getting to know a person. If a candidate does not accept that answer and insists on more frequent contact, it's time for you to either become even less available or break off contact entirely, replacing the candidate with another ASAP. Think of it as a test of the candidate's level of regard or respect for boundaries. It might feel good or flattering if someone strongly pursues you, but how healthy is it if he or she disregards directly stated preferences? You would not want that kind of trend in a relationship.

Meet Infrequently

Another way to juggle having multiple candidates and manage the level of involvement with each is to meet infrequently, getting together not more than once every other week.

When you and a candidate enjoy each other's company, there is a tendency to want more contact. While perfectly understandable, this can lead to premature involvement early in the relationship. It is optimal to meet with each of the three candidates no more than every other week. Meeting at this rate allows for enough contact to maintain an interest, connection, and dialogue, while creating a time buffer that enables you to process your experience with each of the candidates.

A number of apprentices, when considering this guideline, have raised concerns about the possibility of candidates losing interest. This concern creates internal pressure to meet more frequently. Experience has revealed that if a candidate is interested in you, he or she is likely to find that the extended time in between contacts heightens the anticipation of meeting with you again. If the feelings the candidate has for you are genuine, he or she will wait. Remember, you want a relationship for life, one that will endure. Don't you want somebody who can withstand some frustration? Besides, aren't you worth waiting for? Unfortunately, some of you may not be sure and may feel compelled to give in to meeting more often. Consider this: making decisions out of guilt, fear, anxiety, or desperation is based on insecurity, which affects objectivity and reasoning ability. You would leave yourself vulnerable to making decisions for the wrong reasons, increasing the likelihood of a poor outcome.

Vivien, a woman in her early forties, had been divorced for over one and a half years and expressed little interest in meeting men. It did not take long for her to disclose her terror about entering the dating scene, having been out of it "for a long, long time." When she started the Apprenticeship to Love program and met her first candidate, he began to call her frequently. Though she quickly realized he "wasn't her type," she liked the attention. Further conversations revealed that she was relieved that someone could be interested in her. She was afraid that he would stop being interested in her if she didn't make herself available. Having come from a loveless marriage in which she was blamed for the poor relationship, Vivien discovered that much of her anxiety was due to "baggage" from her marriage. She could hear her husband's abusive words and realized that they were his rationalizations for having extramarital affairs and did not have anything to do with her. Vivien discovered that she felt like she couldn't say "no" to her candidate because she lacked self-confidence. By setting the necessary limits with this candidate, Vivien began to challenge old perceptions she had about herself. She learned new behavior that portrayed her improved sense of self. Vivien asserted, "I don't have to settle for just any man. I want someone who wants me 'as is.'"

Feelings of insecurity are neither new nor unusual for anybody. They are usually based on experiences from the past and feelings that get triggered by current circumstances. Take charge of these feelings that can get in the way by identifying, assessing, and addressing them in the current context. This is where a coach can be invaluable in helping you think about and separate what is going on in the present from difficult or painful memories that may be fueling a sense of vulnerability. Recovery from past relationships and misfortunes requires new actions and fresh options in dealing with the difficult feelings that may arise. Like Vivien, refusing to let insecurities dictate decisions gives you the curative experience you need, letting you know that the past does not have to dictate the present. Setting the needed limits in meeting with candidates is an action that enables you to update and reprogram outdated feelings and views about yourself.

Meet on Random Days

Another way to keep the relationship with each candidate at a manageable level is to be sure to meet the candidate on random days so that a particular day or time doesn't become regarded as special. We're all creatures of habit. If you go out with a candidate on the same day several times in a row, there is the tendency to think of that day as special for the two of you. Meeting on different days helps you to avoid this problem. Going out on a weekend night, especially on a Saturday, tends to hold particular significance in our culture, so make it a point to also meet on weekdays. Declining to go out on a weekend night by saying that you have other plans also sends a message to the candidate not to take things for granted or to make certain assumptions about the relationship with you.

Replacing Candidates

It is wise to replace the candidate you've been dating the longest, if you are unlikely to choose him or her for exclusive involvement. The longer you date a person, the closer and more familiar you are likely to feel toward each other. While it is not true in all cases, it certainly is in most. When this is not the case, one needs to ask, "Why not?" The answer tells you something about the other person, the relationship, and you. Does the other person seem bored and disinterested on dates? If you make an effort to be a little bit more engaging, does he or she respond? If not, it could be that the other person does not feel an emotional connection with you. Don't spend a lot of time trying to change the other person. Move on to the next candidate. You want somebody who likes and wants to be with you—someone who has an affinity toward you. That kind of connection is the basis of any good relationship. It is also an important ingredient in developing intimacy.

Experiencing Disinterest

What if you're the one who doesn't experience an interest in the other person? Is this the case with only this particular candidate? Ask questions of yourself that will help isolate the reason(s) for your lack of interest. Maybe it is simply that you have very little in common. Or maybe the candidate reminds you too much of your former wife, husband, or love partner and you didn't realize it at first. That you would gravitate towards a familiar type of person is understandable, but the similarity can create confusion and an emotional reaction in you, such as feeling numb when you are with that individual. If you become aware of this or any other less-than-preferable reaction, look for further objective information that helps explain your response. To simply dismiss the candidate because of an initial emotional reaction could mean you are walking away from a potentially viable candidate. Of course, it is also possible that you are responding to undesirable traits in the candidate not yet exhibited. You may be instinctually pulling away emotionally. Either way it would be wise for you to know by taking the time to assess the nature of a questionable gut reaction. This is a way of taking care of yourself well.

If you find that, for whatever reason, the other person feels better about the relationship than you do and wants to evolve to the next level, state outright that you do not feel the same way. You might even be able to maintain the acquaintance or develop a friendship when both of you know the limitations of the relationship. However, it is important that this person be removed from the position of being a candidate. It is good practice for you to be as straightforward in your communications as possible, but please be kind and sensitive to the other person's feelings. The deposed candidate may not like or feel good to hear that there is no "next step" to the relationship.

Avoid Having Sex with Candidates

You can certainly appreciate how much more complicated the situation would be if there had been sexual involvement. Thus, I underscore the guideline to avoid having sex with a candidate. Having sex immediately advances the relationship and makes it difficult to manage. Some apprentices have found extreme relief in this guideline, others great frustration and annoyance. Rarely has anyone disputed its accuracy. When sex becomes part of the relationship, at least one of the participants will believe that the relationship has evolved to the next level. Problems arise when this is only true for one and not for the other or when an emotional attachment is formed prematurely. The experienced connection often is not based on reason. An emotional attachment can be formed between people who may not be right or good for each another.

Della was managing her three candidates fairly well until she met Bill. She had been networking for several months, and he was the best candidate she had met thus far. He quickly replaced one of the three men already in her program and made a stellar rise to the number-one position. She liked Bill and liked how she felt when she was with him. They had great chemistry. They had a lot of fun together and did interesting things on their dates. The relationship was physical from the onset, and when they had sex by the fourth date, Della was not surprised and even welcomed it. Della felt like there was a magnet pulling her toward Bill, and sex only affirmed how good she felt when she was with him. She dropped the other two candidates so that she could spend more time with Bill. Their relationship took a greater sexual focus, with less time devoted to having lengthy talks about each other. As the novelty of the sexual relationship passed and there was increased time to talk about more details of their respective lives, Della became increasingly aware that Bill actually wasn't as intelligent or as interesting as she thought he was. So much of the focus was on being sexual that she had not taken the time to see that they lacked other things in common. When Della broke off the relationship, Bill was both surprised and hurt, thinking that their relationship had a future.

Interestingly, Della's experience is the opposite of what many people expect—women are more likely to form an attachment to a partner after having sex. Yet it is a reminder that men form bonds and can get hurt, too. Della had been swept up by feelings which, understandably, she liked and did not want to stop. In some situations, emotions can be like mind-altering substances; they intoxicate, loosen up inhibitions, and cloud judgment. Della was drawn to some very attractive but limited qualities of Bill. It felt good to be with Bill, and Della wanted to continue feeling that way. Della felt closer to Bill in the beginning because she felt excited, pleased, and satisfied, but that did not mean that they were right for each other. Other important attributes were missing in the relationship. Della and Bill could not scale back to a friendship because Bill wanted more than Della was able to give.

Della never meant to "use" Bill, but it is understandable how he could have ended up feeling that way. Introducing sex into a relationship raises expectations for at least one participant, if not both, as it is often experienced as an expression of emotional intimacy. In a healthy marriage or other deeply committed relationship, making love is a way of affirming the relationship, connecting and communicating emotionally, and much more. Sex is a dynamic component of a love relationship. But all of that happens when a relationship has evolved to a certain level of intimacy. Introducing sex prematurely often creates faulty assumptions about the union, leading to inevitable tensions and somebody getting hurt.

Keep Replacing Candidates

The longer you are in a relationship, the more likely you are to experience pressure to have sex. One way to limit this complication is to keep replacing candidates. Besides, your goal is to include several generations of candidates in your program. Replacing candidates not only limits your level of involvement, but affords you the opportunity to keep meeting new people. This process is a kind of numbers game. You have to meet a certain number of people until you find the person who is most suited for you. Keep looking for new and different opportunities to meet candidates. You want to go out with a wide spectrum of individuals, the more and different the better. Be sure to look for what is positive and interesting in each person, as it will allow you to have a better time. It doesn't matter if you conclude fairly quickly that he or she is not right for you. You want to experience and explore the different positive human attributes that make up that person. Think of the attributes that you like and are drawn to as gifts that please you in the experience. Some people have one or two gifts while others have many more. Everybody has positive qualities available that you can enjoy in the course of the meeting. Don't forget, this is practice for you, as you are in training. You are getting skilled at making contact, engaging, and interacting with potential candidates and feeling increasingly comfortable in the process. The pros and cons of each person will become visible more quickly, and amazingly, you instinctively begin to look for and choose more of the kind of candidates you prefer. The more potential candidates you meet, the more skilled you become, feeling more confident and effective in your efforts. This process is fundamental in managing the degree of emotional attachment between you and the candidates included in your program. It is also how you will ultimately meet and know that you have met the kind of person that is right for you.

Michael had no problem meeting new candidates for his program. He was in his fifties, good-looking, socially outgoing, financially secure, and had been divorced for several years. In fact, he had met and replaced quite a few candidates over the course of several months. Donna had been his number-one candidate for the longest period of time, and Michael found himself wanting to have the greatest amount of contact with her. He had been thinking of dropping the other two candidates and entering an exclusive relationship with Donna. However, he found himself noticing and thinking about how Donna could say and do things that annoyed him. He began to look at her with a more critical eye and noticed an ever-increasing number of traits about her that he found unappealing. Michael concluded that he had not been realistic in his past assessment of Donna and moved her from the number-one slot to number three, planning to replace her as soon as he met a fourth candidate.

At first glance, it might appear that Michael simply took a closer look at Donna and was clearer in his assessment of her, which would be reasonable. When asked about his sudden change of heart, Michael realized that his shift in feelings about Donna did seem rather abrupt and similar to his other experiences with women. He had gotten a divorce after his wife of thirty years announced that she was a lesbian and was moving in with her lover. He had been shocked and devastated. Since then, Michael often felt unsure whether he could ever trust a woman again. Childhood experiences further complicated his feelings about women's trustworthiness. He and his two older siblings were raised by his father; his mother left the family and moved out of state when Michael was five years old. His father was overwhelmed by the needs of three children, worked many hours to support the family, and left the older siblings to watch over Michael. Children were left to raise children, resulting in Michael experiencing huge gaps in his emotional and relational development. His closeness with Donna and contemplation of having an exclusive relationship with her triggered a sense of vulnerability, which to him meant being inevitably abandoned again.

Donna could sense that Michael had distanced himself from her. She asked if anything was wrong, and he denied there was. Trusting her intuition about Michael and the relationship that they had together, Donna reminded him how positive things had been between them and observed how he had pulled away then asked about the change in him. Michael could have given her a lame excuse, but he didn't want to. Instead he told her that lately he had been feeling "cornered" in their relationship and needed some "space." Instead of Donna being angry, critical, or rejecting, he found her to be receptive, understanding, and supportive. Donna told Michael how important it was to her for him to tell her whatever he needed so that they could have an unencumbered relationship. If he needed more time for himself, Michael was free to do what he needed. Michael realized that Donna cared for him and that he would be walking away from a "classy lady." He felt relieved, grateful, and closer to Donna for the way she had dealt with him. He decided to drop the other two candidates to more deeply explore his relationship with Donna.

Donna was a smart and "classy" lady in the way she handled Michael. She sensed that Michael was pulling away and, knowing his history, suspected that his past may have had something to do with it. Donna was dealing with Michael in an honest, direct way. The fact that Michael responded favorably was good for both of them. If he had not, she would be better off with the relationship ending. You don't need perfection in a relationship, just "workability"! The way to know if you are in a workable relationship is if differences are resolved amicably. Both partners in the relationship should be open-minded, willing to take the time to try to understand what the other person is saying and wanting to find constructive solutions that are not at the expense of either person. To do this, a person needs to be able to acknowledge his or her own strengths and limitations. Remember, everybody has issues to work out. As I've said, people who can't acknowledge having any problems, weaknesses, or limitations have even bigger issues. Relationships are only as strong as each member's capacity to deal with personal frailties and shortcomings. It is important to be on the lookout for a candidate who seems to know how to handle problems between you or is willing to learn. Without this trait, the relationship is likely to fail.

Exhausting Your Social Circle

With all the meeting and replacing of candidates that is being suggested, it is likely that you will eventually run out of candidates to meet from your social circle. Don't worry, this is normal. After all, if there were plenty of available, higher level candidates to meet in your current social circle, you probably would be going out with them already. It is time to apply the principles that you learned in chapter 2 to help you break into new social and professional circles. If you don't, managing the relationship with the current candidates will become more difficult due to the increased emotional pressures that normally occur with time. While you want to avoid discharging candidates from your program before finding a replacement, the remaining one or two might become undeservedly important simply because there is nobody else. Remember, when you meet a new person, you potentially have access to all of his or her friends, family, and colleagues, one of which could become your next candidate or introduce you to a person who will.

Wall of Doubt

Any new situation requires innovative thinking and unfamiliar actions. This is true, for example, when you are trying to gain entry into a new social or professional context. The more unfamiliar the situation, the harder we need to work to adapt and be effective. It is possible that in the midst of making efforts in your Apprenticeship to Love program, you will encounter one or more emotional barriers in yourself. This "wall of doubt" is normal, and you must learn to scale it. Sometimes, it comes early in the program, and occasionally, it takes you by surprise just when you think that you're doing pretty well. What is this wall of doubt? It can take many forms. You might find yourself thinking, can I really find a person who makes me happy? Am I attractive enough? Am I good enough to go to that social gathering? Am I interesting enough? You can end up feeling so inadequate or vulnerable that your efforts can come to a standstill. You can overcome this. Take the time to sort through your feelings, identifying and objectively evaluating the basis for them. If you do, you are likely to see that these concerns are rooted in negative judgment and insecurity. There is a strong chance that these insecurities are not new to you and are rooted in the past. Remind yourself that you can't change the past and that it has little or nothing to do with what is going on in the present. This repeated exposure to old, difficult feelings you were avoiding will help desensitize you to them and allow mastery over them. Speak with your coach who can shed some light on the situation by asking the kind of questions that will help you sort through your experience. Seeing the current situation with greater clarity enables you to manage your feelings better and make more effective decisions about what to do. That is called healing through progress.

Julie was feeling discouraged. Every man she met turned out to be a "fixer-upper." She was tired of being in relationships with men who didn't appreciate her or her efforts with them. She felt used, cheated, and scared that she would never be able to find someone with whom to be happy. While talking to her coach about her fears, Julie recalled that her father always seemed to make excuses for her mother, who was frequently depressed and uninvolved. Julie's mother seemed to take no interest in her, despite Julie's efforts to please and be noticed by her. Julie and her siblings turned to their father for their needs because their mother was always struggling just to function. Julie speculated that maybe she had emulated her father, whom she loved but pitied because he had to take care of her mother. Julie questioned why her mother never seemed to love her, thinking herself lacking in something, not comprehending that her mother simply wasn't available to anybody because of her depression. This realization shed new light on the root of her self-doubt. Julie didn't have to fix somebody in order to feel worthwhile. She was worthwhile already.

Like many people, Julie was living her life on autopilot. She did not think about cause and effect. By talking to her coach, Julie was able to identify a recurring destructive theme in her relationships, which was limiting her choice of a life partner. Julie became aware that this was not an accident but was rooted in incorrect conclusions about her own childhood experiences. As a child, Julie was in no position to understand that her mother was too depressed to show her love. Julie had blamed herself. Being the one always responsible for everything in a relationship with a man was a way in which Julie tried to extract love from her partner. Trying to love a man under these terms set her up to feel unhappy and unfulfilled. Julie decided to change the rules in her search for love. She consciously changed her working premise to acknowledge that she was already lovable and did not have to prove it to her partner. Julie realized that she had been letting candidates choose her and that she needed to be more involved in the selection process.

Selecting Which Candidate to Replace Is Supposed to Get Harder, Not Easier

In the beginning of your personal program, it is likely that you will find it easy to know which candidates to replace. As the program progresses and you become better at meeting and selecting candidates who have an increasing number of the traits you desire (I will call them higher level candidates), the decision-making process is likely to become more difficult. This is actually a positive sign that you are doing a good job in your selection; each successive generation should include a candidate that is closer to the kind of person with whom you want a long-term relationship. If this is not the case, then it is time for you to take a closer look at your selection process. Like Julie, you could be attracted to candidates with a pattern of traits that is not working out well. Ask yourself if you keep feeling the same way about the candidates you choose. What could it be about a candidate that makes you feel like that? Is it a trait or a behavior? If you can identify the problem, you can work toward a solution. Keep in mind that the problem can be in you, which can be a good thing since you are more likely to have direct access and control of yourself than other people.

Emotional Affairs

Whatever you do, avoid "emotional affairs" as they are not harmless and will get in the way of your success. An emotional affair is a relationship that exists in your mind but is not put into effect with the other person. It can occur with or without the knowledge of the object of your desire. The love object of the emotional affair is usually unavailable because of marriage, being committed to someone else, or other circumstances. Because the relationship is not actualized, a person idealizes the love object and the imagined relationship, comparing others to this "perfect" standard. Real people and relationships pale by comparison. Because the feeling can be so strong, other relationships are passed over or avoided, as if one is being faithful to the imagined partner. This phenomenon is actually a psychological protective mechanism, even though it can cause a great deal of pain. The unrealized emotional affair is like a protective cloak; it shields the person from the potential hurt associated with real relationships. Of course, the person having the emotional affair suffers the frustration and emptiness of unrealized love, but in his or her mind, it is better, because this pain is self-created. Even though it's hard to compete with an idealized fantasy, a real person has a lot more to offer and real relationships are ultimately a lot more satisfying.

When a Candidate Is Right for You, You Will Know It

As the Apprenticeship to Love program progresses and you have processed several generations of candidates, your experiences enable you to become increasingly effective in more quickly identifying people and relationships that are better suited to you. You begin to know and understand which traits and characteristics are more satisfying because you have had the opportunity to see and experience what works for you and what doesn't, what is important and what isn't. Keep in mind that you are not looking for *the* right person. Rather you are looking for *your type of person*, which is much easier to find.

As your own interpersonal skills grow, you will become better prepared for a more exclusive relationship. Somewhere in the process of meeting candidates, you will find one with whom you are relating in a very special and positive way. When you find yourself increasingly drawn to this person and this person wants to have a more involved relationship with you, it may be time to discharge the other two candidates and temporarily halt the search for additional ones. You then explore the possibilities of this relationship on a full-time basis and enter the stage of "when three become one."

Chapter Review:
The Art of Prospecting for Love
With Three Candidates

- Form a controllable level of involvement with each of the candidates.
- Maintain infrequent contact with each candidate, speaking every few days at the most.
- Meet infrequently
- Meet on Random Days
- Replace the candidate you've been dating the longest if you are unlikely to choose him or her for exclusive involvement.
- You want somebody who likes and wants to be with you—someone who has an affinity toward you.
- If there is disinterest in the relationship either by you or the candidate, take the time to find out why that is.
- Avoid having sex with candidates.
- Keep replacing candidates. Finding one that is best suited for you is a numbers game that involves meeting a certain amount of new people.
- You are likely to exhaust your social circle and will need to break into a new one to find additional candidates.
- Hitting a "wall of doubt" about yourself is normal, and you must learn to scale it.
- As the program progresses, selecting which candidate to replace is supposed to get harder, not easier.
- Beware of "emotional affairs" as they are not harmless and will get in the way of your success.
- When a candidate is right for you, you will know it.
- If you are not having fun, rethink your approach.

Chapter Four
When Three Candidates Are
Narrowed Down to One

What if you like a particular candidate more and more with each passing week? In fact, you look forward to seeing, speaking to, and being with him or her over the other two and have thoughts of having an exclusive relationship. How do you know if it is the right time to have an exclusive relationship with this person? What are you looking for and how will you know when you find it? How will you know if this person is right for you? The process of answering these questions brings you to the next level in your Apprenticeship to Love.

When Considering an Exclusive Relationship

First let us consider if it is time to have an exclusive relationship. Before discharging the other two candidates answer the following questions:
- Does this special person want to get to know you as intently as you want to get to know him or her?
- Is this candidate truly available (i.e., not involved in another romantic relationship)? If not, is he or she willing to end the other relationship(s) entirely?
- If the relationship works out, are you ready to take the next step?
- Can you afford to take the risk of the relationship *not* working out?

If the answer is "yes" to all of the above questions, you are ready to explore an exclusive relationship with this particular candidate. If not, continue meeting and replacing candidates in your program until you are ready and find someone you really like who is ready too. Rather than thinking of this as *the* decision to make in your personal program, it is best regarded as *a* decision among many in your journey. You are simply moving to the next step of a relationship to see what is and is not there. Like before, you want to have fun and enjoy the process while letting reason and objectivity determine your conclusions.

Learning About Your Candidate

There are so many things to learn about this candidate, which makes for a very interesting and exciting experience. The views that you have held about him or her up to now are best regarded as initial impressions. The only true way to know a person is to spend time with him or her in different contexts. The more diverse the experiences that you have with this candidate, the more knowledgeable you become as to what life would be like with him or her. Simple, everyday kinds of situations can be very telling. For example, how does this candidate interact with people in general (e.g., the cabbie, waitress, or other service person in your presence)? Is it with a sense of regard or respect? How generous is he or she? Casual interactions say many things about the candidate's character and attitudes about others (and you in the future). Who are this candidate's friends and how does he or she relate to them? Remember, people tend to surround themselves with others who reflect similar values. Are there any close friends in the picture or are they all casual acquaintances? Do you like them and vice versa? After all, these are the people who would encompass a portion of your social life if you and your candidate stay together.

Assessing the Time Together

How does it feel to spend longer, more consistent periods of time with this person? Do you feel comfortable in his or her presence, like being with a good friend? Is the feeling mutual? Do you laugh together? Can you talk about more personal subjects and have it be a dialogue rather than a one-sided conversation? You are learning about the "fit" between the two of you, how you two are together and with each other. Keep in mind that there are some people who tend to be shy or reserved when around others less familiar. Such individuals can "warm up" socially after a while. If the candidate remains emotionally distant, it may simply reflect his or her character style, which is usually stable. Don't try to change this person. The candidate has to be good enough "as is," with all the strengths and weaknesses that exist. While it is true that we all can improve ourselves, entering a relationship based on the premise that you will change the other person is heartache in the making. What you are looking for in a relationship is influence, not control. You want the other person to bring out the best in you and vice versa. Because of your differences, you two expose each other to new possibilities in ways of being that can create opportunities for personal growth, as shown in the following example.

Harry is a good person and a successful lawyer in his early sixties. A widower for three years, he only began dating again in the last twelve months. His deceased wife didn't seem to mind his gruff demeanor and sarcastic wit. After all, he was a loyal, loving husband who was very generous and supportive. The women he was dating did not see Harry in the same light. Harry was attracted to "classy," intelligent women who did not want to continue dating him after a couple of outings. Harriet was different. She liked Harry's intelligence and wry sense of humor. She understood that Harry's persona reflected his humble beginnings in the inner city and did not take his rough edges personally. Because she wasn't intimidated by him, Harriet pointed out to Harry when he crossed over the line of good taste in his humor or was being hurtful rather than funny. He respected Harriet and knew she was caring in her comments. Harry appreciated her taking the time and having the interest to give him helpful information that nobody else had. After all, he wasn't trying to be mean or crass, just funny. Harry was drawn closer to Harriet as he felt like he was becoming a better person as a result of being with her. Harriet understood what Harry's wife had seen in him and felt fortunate to have met him.

Feeling Good in a Relationship

Good, loving relationships make you feel good about yourself and can inspire you. You like the way you feel and want more of that experience. You want to look into your partner's eyes, which become like emotional mirrors, and like who and what you see in the reflection. The experience tells you a great deal about how the other person feels about you. Look closely. Are you seeing how he or she feels or how you want to be seen? If they are one and the same, it is a good sign. Like the last example, we can say that Harriet inspired Harry to try to be a better person. He wanted to present more of the person Harriet envisioned him as being. This is a winning combination for both Harry and Harriet.

During one of their discussions, Harriet shared with Harry her interest in writing short stories for children and of a dream to publish some of her writings. Harry asked to read some of her work, expressed how much he liked the stories, and encouraged her to publish them. Harriet appreciated Harry's comments but questioned the quality of her productions. Viewing Harriet's comments as a reflection of her modesty but realizing his limited expertise on the matter, Harry suggested and then encouraged Harriet to join a writer's group comprised of people who are in a position to help her develop her craft. Though Harriet was aware of such groups, she had felt intimidated at the prospects of applying to join one. Buoyed by Harry's comments and support, Harriet decided to research and apply to a local writer's group.

Maybe Harriet would have pursued the writer's group without Harry's support, but you can see how his input tipped the scale toward her taking positive action. We are witness to a combination of self-interest and concern for what is important for the other. Be on the lookout for this in your relationship as it is a feature to be prized and promotes mutual personal growth.

Introducing Your Interests to the Candidate

This is the time to introduce this candidate to the activities and interests that excite you and for you to try out his or hers. It would be convenient if the other person liked most of the same things you do, but that is usually not the case. What is more important is how each of you relates to and deals with each other's different preferences.

The opera season was just beginning, and Hillary wanted to share this passion of hers with Mark. Though he had never seen a live opera performance, Mark told her of having heard some on the radio and TV, at which time he would usually switch the channel. Hillary told Mark that the experience is very different when at the opera house and that not all opera is the same. Hillary asked Mark if he would be willing to try going to one with her. When he agreed, she carefully picked a popular opera for him to sample. After the show, Mark thanked her for the opportunity but candidly stated that he still did not like opera. Though disappointed, Hillary understood that opera is not for everyone and continued to attend future productions with her friends as she had before, with Mark's blessings.

The next best thing to having the same interest is supporting each other's participation in your respectively enjoyed activities. At the very least, it is best not to interfere.

Jeff loves baseball. He is an avid fan who loves to talk about his favorite baseball team and goes to games at the stadium where he holds season tickets. Pam thinks grown men throwing a ball around and hitting it with a stick is silly. She really likes Jeff and initially went to games with him, knowing just how much he liked baseball. Now that they have been going out for a while, she has stopped going to the stadium and is becoming increasingly annoyed by just how many games there are in a season. To make matters worse, the baseball team Jeff loves has made it to the playoffs, extending the season. Lately, Jeff and Pam end up arguing before each game. Jeff feels Pam is trying to make him feel guilty for going. Pam thinks Jeff is being selfish and uncaring by leaving her alone, despite the fact that he has repeatedly asked her to go with him.

If Jeff stopped going to baseball games, it is likely that he would become resentful of Pam. In order for Pam to stay in a relationship with Jeff, she had to develop her own interests and passions and be more understanding of Jeff's. Pam's ex-husband was a "high-maintenance" kind of person who demanded much of her time. Pam was not used to thinking about what interested her. Being with Jeff required her to rethink her own needs, giving her the chance to evolve in ways that made her feel more like her own person. Now Jeff and Pam had to find mutual interests.

Connoisseurs of fine foods, Pam and Jeff loved to try new restaurants and sample culinary delights. They decided to take cooking classes together and reveled in trying new recipes. They cooked together on weekends, inviting their friends for dinner parties to try out their experimentations. When baseball season was in full swing and Jeff knew he would be attending a weekend game, he took the time to research and find a restaurant he and Pam had not been to before and made reservations, creating time together.

Tolerance and Flexibility

Tolerance and flexibility in tandem with regard for each other is what makes having differences feel more manageable in a relationship. Differences introduce new ideas and opportunities, enriching your lives and giving you new viewpoints to consider in your experience. Keep in mind, the more differences that you have between you, the harder you are going to have to work in your relationship. Make sure that there are enough common core interests so that you are not struggling most of the time.

Communication, Consideration, Patience, and Commitment

Any good relationship requires work ... sometimes very hard work. But good ones also bring joy and satisfaction. Survival of the relationship is determined by a willingness of those involved to stay together long enough to work out problems and difficulties that arise. Commitment (or lack thereof) can make or break a relationship.

Gwen and Brian have been dating for six months and agreed to be monogamous in the relationship after three months of dating. Gwen is socially outgoing and has many friends, some of whom are her ex-boyfriends. Though it was difficult for Brian to get used to the idea that he was socializing with some of Gwen's old flames, he adapted when he saw that there didn't appear to be a romantic interest, except with Zachary. While Brian trusted Gwen, he did not like the way Zachary treated him when they socialized. Brian felt that Zachary still had a romantic interest in Gwen and acted as if he was in competition for her. Brian tried to talk to Gwen about his concerns, but she disagreed with his conclusions about

Zachary and reassured Brian he need not be jealous. Gwen had long ago broken off her romantic involvement with Zachary when he refused to stop dating other women during their courtship. Gwen now considered Zachary a good friend because of how supportive he had been during a difficult, prolonged divorce. Brian didn't trust Zachary, seeing him as potentially divisive and told Gwen so. However, he trusted Gwen and decided to not press the issue. Gwen began to pay closer attention to Zachary when she was with him and saw what Brian had been saying. As a friend, she tried to speak to Zachary about it, but he was emphatic in his view that Brian was not right for her. Gwen decided to take a holiday from her friendship with Zachary.

Brian's patience paid off. He knew Gwen was oblivious to Zachary's intent and was frustrated, but Brian was committed to seeing how it would play out. The interchange between Brian and Gwen demonstrated four important components of a good relationship:

1) Honest, direct, constructive communication
2) Consideration of what the other person is saying, even if it is difficult to hear
3) Being patient, giving the other person time to consider and come to his or her own conclusions about the new information
4) Commitment to staying in the relationship and working out their problems

Apologizing With Sincerity

Since everybody makes mistakes, an important trait you want in a relationship with your solo candidate is the ability to apologize. Saying "I'm sorry" with sincerity is a sign of strength, not weakness. Being able to acknowledge your contribution to problems and situations:

- Demonstrates willingness to assume personal responsibility
- Tells the other person that he or she is not being held totally responsible
- Conveys open-mindedness toward finding resolution
- Initiates a process towards reconciling differences
- Paves a pathway towards forgiveness

Conflict handled well in a relationship is reassuring. Because conflict is inevitable in *any* relationship, learning that you have the skills needed to address problems as they arise is an important part of the "fit" between the two of you.

Challenged Objectivity

In the earlier part of your Apprenticeship to Love program, you stopped and took inventory on how the three candidates were fairing, identifying their strengths and weaknesses, and then rank ordered them. At this stage, you are likely to find your objectivity in assessing the relationship with this solo candidate to be more challenged than when you were dating three. That is because your perspective has changed. The more time you spend dating someone and liking the experience, the closer you feel to that person, biasing your perspective. Nevertheless, do take inventory and look at the information you know. Make a list of this candidate's strengths and the things you like about him or her. Now make a list of his or her weaknesses and the things you may have concerns about. How serious are these concerns, and how workable do you see them as being?

Marcie and Clive have been going out exclusively for almost nine months. Marcie loves most things about Clive except his drinking, which he seems to do too much of. When she tries to talk to him about it, he tells her he's just relaxing after a hard day of work and that he has it under control. Clive's breath often smells of alcohol when he comes to see her, and he has several hard liquor drinks "straight up" when he is with her. Marcie's heart tells her Clive is a great guy and to overlook this flaw. Her head is sending all kinds of warning signals that this one flaw is a big one that may be a deal breaker in their relationship.

If Marcie had just met Clive, his drinking may not matter much to her or she could end the relationship without too much heartache. Now that she cares for Clive and feels emotionally connected to him, it is not so easy. Despite what Marcie's heart tells her, if Clive is unwilling to address his drinking problem now, their future is likely to be marred by it. Facts are facts, despite attraction, and these are what relationship decisions need to be based on.

You Don't Have to Decide Alone

While the bottom line in making a decision is yours, you do not have to go through the process of deciding alone. Don't forget your friends! They were there with you before this candidate came into your life, and they know you. One definition of a good friend is a person who will take a chance and tell you things nobody else will, for your own sake. That's the person you want to go to when trying to sort out and evaluate your relationship. A common complaint made by friends of apprentices is being forgotten when a love interest comes into the picture. It's not hard to figure out or understand how this happens. Romance can be intoxicating. However, this is exactly when friendships can help keep you grounded. If you don't have a friend or a coach to help sort through your relationship, go to a licensed counselor who is unbiased and can help you assess your relationship. Remember, this is a trial run to assess your own readiness for a meaningful relationship which is just as important as any information you may find about your candidate. You might already feel in love with this person, but that doesn't mean that you are ready for marriage.

Cynthia had been widowed for a year when she was introduced to Lewis, himself widowed not much longer. The relationship between them progressed fairly quickly, much quicker than Cynthia ever imagined. Lewis was serious, and he let her know of his desire to marry her. Cynthia was serious too but didn't feel ready for such a commitment. Her female friends, some of whom had been alone for a few years, told her she was crazy if she didn't accept. She, herself, didn't like the feeling of being alone at times, but that was the point. She knew she was still in mourning and wasn't sure if she would be accepting Lewis's proposal because of a sense of need rather than want. Even though Cynthia loved Lewis, she told him she was not ready for marriage.

Cynthia made a smart decision not to force herself to do something she was not ready for. Some of you might be concerned that Lewis would not want to wait, causing Cynthia to run the risk of losing him. That is certainly a possibility. Yet if Lewis presses Cynthia to marry, does he really understand, regard, and know how to deal with Cynthia's needs? After all, Cynthia presents herself as a woman who is comfortable with her own ideas and needs a man who appreciates that about her. She simply needs more time to go through the grieving process. If Lewis understands this and is patient, he will be the beneficiary of a partner willingly choosing him. If Cynthia accepts marriage out of fear of losing him, Lewis may not like the outcome.

Free Will in Making a Decision

The concept of free will is very important in relationships (and life for that matter). Nobody likes to feel forced or trapped. Remembering that you have a choice can help you manage anxiety that may surface from time to time in a relationship, particularly during decision-making times. In fact, the healthiest and happiest of relationships are those where the individuals in it are content with their respective lives and choose to be together because they want to be, not because they need to be.

One Cannot Love Enough for Two

It is tremendously rewarding to have someone care about you similarly to the way you care about that person. But what if that is not the case? What if one of you is in love and the other is not? As a teenager, I was advised, "Never love someone that doesn't love you back." That piece of advice is no less true for anyone today. In order for a relationship to be healthy and viable, both of you need to be in love with each other. One person cannot love enough for two, though some have tried unsuccessfully.

Sex Does Not Equal Love

Assessing feelings about a relationship can be challenging when sex becomes part of the relationship too early. Despite how it can feel, sex alone does not equal love. There is a difference between loving the sex and loving the person you are having sex with. How another person really feels about you (and vice versa) is answered by what happens the rest of the time you two are together and not having sex. On the other hand, a lack of physical attraction by either one of you should not be simply dismissed or taken for granted. A lack of physical interest or attraction by one of you can lead to frustration and a sense of rejection for the other.

Becoming Good Friends

Is this candidate becoming a good friend? Good friends like to be together since they have fun. They are helpful and supportive of each other, tolerant of each other's idiosyncrasies, honest and considerate of one another, and willing to work out problems. Not surprisingly, when couples who identified themselves as having been happily married for over thirty-five years were asked what made their relationships successful, the majority cited being each other's best friend as the primary reason.

Sharing Core Values

Do you and this solo candidate share similar values about life, children, religion/spirituality, money, work, etc.? The more core values that you have in common, the better off you are. There will be fewer causes of tension in the future, and you will have greater agreement in goals and pursuits. It is during the current phase of the relationship that you need to be clearest about your views on life and the views of this candidate. Don't assume. Take the time to find out your candidates' thoughts on these important matters. Trying to work it out after the fact can be a recipe for a disaster, for example, imagine telling a love partner after you are married that you don't want to have any (more) children or saying that you will only marry someone of your religion after you have been dating for many months.

Jack and Jill, who live in different cities, have reached a point of monogamy in their relationship. Jack is in his mid-fifties and Jill in her later forties. Both are divorced several years, but Jack's youngest child is in college and Jill's is not yet in high school. While Jack and Jill share many common interests, Jack wants more focused couple involvement and greater spontaneity involving travel. While Jill values these interests, she is committed to raising her youngest child and also to her evolving career. They did not see their different stages in career and parenting as reconcilable, and they decided to remain friends but cease to be romantic partners.

Maybe another couple could see a workable solution to this dilemma, but Jack and Jill did not. By acknowledging their different priorities and limitations, Jack and Jill were able to recognize that they would not be a good fit for each other. They didn't have to judge or be angry with the other person. Both spared themselves (and each other) unnecessary pain.

Asking Yourself Some Necessary, Tough Questions

While it would not be appropriate to ask or make any conclusions about the future of a relationship early on, it is most certainly important to wonder about it with the passage of time. Oftentimes, you may get a sense by the language used, for example, by references made to events in the long-distant future. However, if after six months to a year,[3] you still do not know, you have to ask yourself if it is because of you or the other person. If you are the reluctant one, ask the following questions.

- What am I worried about, and is there any basis for my worry?
- Is there anything that I can do (and would be willing to do) that would make me want to be with this person for the rest of my life?
- Is there anything that he/she can do (and might be willing to do) that would make a difference for me?
- Am I being reasonable to think that I can change my mind about this person?

Be honest with yourself and the other person. You will be sorrier if you are not. Remember, you are a work in progress

---

3   A number of apprentices have expressed to me that six months is too short a time to determine the long-term viability of a relationship. My experience is that if after one year's time, an apprentice or a candidate is not sure whether the other person is lifetime material, more time is not likely to help. Keep in mind that there is a difference between liking each other's company and wanting to commit to a relationship.

and there will be others. If it is the other person who is still not sure after that time, it's time for you to either set a limit or start looking for three new candidates.

Rick and Marsha had been going out exclusively for almost a year. Both were enjoying each other's company, which led Rick to ask Marsha to move into his apartment. After some thought, Marsha stated that she loved Rick, but she did not want to move in with him unless she knew that their future was going to be together. Rick was stunned; he didn't know if he was ready to consider their long-term future. After considerable thought, weighing the pros and cons of their relationship, Rick concluded that Marsha was everything that he could want in a life partner. He proposed marriage to Marsha.

In this situation, Marsha was confident in her values and personal choices, which guided her in setting a limit. Had Marsha compromised her fundamental values to be with Rick, it would have been the first of many such compromises to come.

Being Practical and Realistic

It is very important that we be practical and realistic when making a decision about a relationship. Remind yourself the relationship is what it is and it isn't what it isn't; either it works well or it doesn't. Base your determination of strengths and weaknesses on facts, not needs or hopes for change. If something is good, it can withstand scrutiny. Noticeable imperfections do not have to detract from the overall goodness of the person or the relationship. We are looking for the "workability" of a relationship, not perfection.

Identifying a Good, Healthy Relationship

How are you going to know if the relationship is on solid ground? When the following three conditions occur:

1. Being with the candidate brings out the best in you.
2. Being with you brings out the best in the candidate.
3. Life is better for both of you as a consequence of being together.

What Next?

Once you have found a good relationship, what happens next? Enjoyment! Usually you and the candidate will progress to the point of wanting a deeper involvement. The level of intimacy will strengthen, and both of you will wish to become life partners. More will be said on this topic in chapter 7, "From Apprentice to Marital Partner." If the commitment to marriage is not evident (within a year, maximum), address this matter with your solo candidate, ending the relationship if needed. Either the other person wants to be with you, or not. Do not try to force the other person, as you want someone to freely choose to be with you. If the relationship ends, reinstate the Apprenticeship to Love program. By now you know how to do it and understand that it works. This break up is likely painful, but you are in control of your life and now have a better idea of what works in a successful relationship and what does not.

The fact that women and men think differently in many regards has long been acknowledged in our society. This fact is neither good nor bad; it "just is." To deny it or not take it into account in relationships is a big mistake. The next two chapters will be devoted to men and women separately, addressing different considerations as it relates to the Apprenticeship to Love program.

Chapter Review:
When Three Candidates Are Narrowed Down to One

When considering an exclusive relationship, ask yourself:

- Does this special person want to get to know me as intently as I want to get to know him or her?
- Is this candidate truly available (i.e., not involved in another romantic relationship)? If not, is he or she willing to end the other relationship(s) entirely?
- If the relationship works out, am I ready to take the next step?
- Can I afford to take the risk of the relationship *not* working out?

What to keep in mind when dating one candidate:

- You will learn a great deal about your special candidate by spending time with him or her in different contexts.
- Good, loving relationships make you feel good about yourself.
- Tolerance and flexibility in tandem with regard for each other is what makes having differences feel more manageable in a relationship.
- Any good relationship requires work ... sometimes very hard work.
- Survival of any relationship is determined by a willingness of those involved to stay together long enough to work out problems and difficulties that arise.
- Since everybody makes mistakes, an important trait you want in a relationship with your solo candidate is the ability to apologize.
- Assessing the relationship with this solo candidate

can be very challenging. Turn to your friends and coach when trying to sort out and evaluate your relationship.

- Take inventory and look at the information you know, making a list of this candidate's strengths and weaknesses.
- The healthiest and happiest of relationships are those where the individuals in it are content with their respective lives and choose to be together because they want to be, not because they need to be.
- One cannot love enough for two.
- Sex does not equal love.
- You and this solo candidate should be becoming good friends who share core values. Are you?

Three conditions that let you know the relationship is on solid ground:

- Being with the candidate brings out the best in you.
- Being with you brings out the best in the candidate.
- Life is better for both of you as a consequence of being together.

If after six months to a year you are still undecided about the future of the relationship, it is time to ask some tough, necessary questions.

Chapter 5
Just for Women

Women didn't need scientists to conclude that there are differences in the way men and women think. They have known this all along. Some women, however, have been more effective in using that information to work in their favor than others. This chapter is written for women apprentices, providing conceptual guidelines, behavioral suggestions, and insight into the male psyche that will help you assume the proper posture towards male candidates and would-be candidates. You will learn how to be more effective in your interactions with men so that in the end, *you* will be the one choosing your love partner for life.

**"I didn't know I could choose to have a relationship with a man. I always thought the man was supposed to choose me."
—All too many women**

Dispelling the myth that a man is supposed to choose the woman for a relationship is the first step in empowering women in the Apprenticeship to Love program. Actually, it is more of a misunderstanding than a myth. Because men are traditionally expected to initiate contact with the woman, some think that it is therefore up to *him* to choose. This is simply inaccurate as either person can decide what will or will not happen. Let us consider two different scenarios.

Scenario I: Linda was at a benefit hosted by a local chapter of an environmental group when she spotted Charles whom she found attractive and who was not sporting a wedding ring. She positioned herself in the room so that she would be in his line of view. She looked in his general direction, and when she saw Charles looking at her, she held his glance for a moment and smiled slightly before looking elsewhere. While talking to various people in the room, Linda made sure she was partially facing Charles when possible, rather than having her back to him. When it came time to sit for the lecture portion of the program, Linda made sure she was alone and chose a chair at the end of an aisle, leaving a seat empty next to her. Charles politely asked if the seat was taken, and she responded, "No," and smiled slightly. When Charles made a comment about the speaker, she responded in a friendly manner. They began to converse about the topic they came to listen to and the discussion carried over to the reception afterwards.

In this scenario, Charles may have uttered the first words in their interchange, but Linda had clearly set the stage for their meeting. She knew that many things get communicated in the initial interactions between a man and a woman, and she wanted to send Charles the right signals. For example, eye contact is a very powerful communicator. Linda conveyed a sense of interest towards Charles by visually engaging him for a moment. Her smile told Charles that she liked what she saw. By making sure that she positioned herself partly facing Charles, she conveyed a sense of being approachable. Had Charles remained silent, unsure of whether to initiate contact once he sat next to Linda, she still could have looked at him at the end of the talk and warmly asked, "Wasn't he a great speaker?" creating yet another opportunity for dialogue between them. Linda was taking action to provide a consistent message. If Linda found that she liked Charles in the course of their interchanges, she could have complimented Charles on his tie and/or moved in closer to him while talking. All these actions are meant to be engaging and erase confusion for Charles as to what Linda's intent is. Who chose whom?

Scenario II: Linda spotted Charles at the social function, liked the way he looked, saw no wedding ring on his finger, and decided to meet him. She waited until Charles went to get a beverage, walked over to do the same, and initiated a conversation with him about the speaker they were about to hear, looking at Charles warmly and engagingly as she did so.

Here Linda took a more direct action in meeting Charles. Her interest was in creating an opportunity to find out more about him. She did not know if he was married or whether she would even want to see Charles again. She was simply exploring. Linda was not invested in the outcome and did not have a high expectation. She was meeting and greeting and felt like she could afford to take the risk making overtures to Charles.

Which one of Linda's actions can you see yourself doing? Either one would be preferable to not doing anything at all. Maybe you can see yourself doing some of both, depending on the situation. *But what if Charles didn't respond or worse, what if Charles responded poorly?* Many women are intimidated by the prospect of looking desperate, feeling embarrassed, or being judged poorly because of their actions. Ironically, most men are grateful when a woman gives a clear welcome signal to him that she wants to meet or when she initiates contact. Men are no less scared of rejection than women. Many men view a poor response from a woman as a kind of statement or question about their masculinity! You can see why you will have more success if you let a man know you are interested in being met than if you don't.

Don't Give Away Your Power

Many women automatically give men way too much power and then become intimidated by it. Though the view is slowly shifting, most of the world still views men as the main source for leadership, strength, and change. Yet men won't even ask for directions when lost. Many men abhor showing vulnerability as they view it as weakness and look to women for emotional direction and guidance. A woman who understands just how easily bruised the male ego is can engage men by assuming a safe, inviting, nurturing posture. The more interested the woman is in what the man is saying and encouraging of him to speak, the more attractive she will appear to him. The more experience you have with men, the less intimidated you will surely be as you realize they have their vulnerabilities and insecurities too. They just hide it more and deal with it differently.

Confidence through Experience

The Apprenticeship to Love program is designed to give you confidence through experience, not unlike a shy woman becoming a teacher and finding her voice in the classroom. Through practice and repeated exposure, she becomes more comfortable with herself and the students and even learns to speak in front of parents and other teachers as well. The same is true of any person in any new situation; practice gives you mastery. In this program, you are being trained to become more comfortable in the presence of men, in engaging them, and in learning about them. Because you are a student, you are expected to feel nervous at times, make mistakes, and not feel competent on the subject of men and relationships. Toward that end, start to look at men as the subject of your personal study. See which men respond to you based on what you say, what you do, and how you do it. If you let yourself, you can have a lot of fun in the process.

> People often say, "beauty is in the eye of the beholder," and I say that the most liberating thing about beauty is realizing that YOU are the beholder. This empowers us to find beauty in places where others have not dared to look, including inside ourselves!
>
> —Selma Hayek

Some of you may have become distant from your feminine side through years of neglect or non-expression within a marriage. Some women are even reluctant to consider meeting men, even though they want to, because they question their ability to attract the opposite sex. It's time to reclaim your feminine side, as it is a vibrant part of you that is very attractive to men. Yes, men are visually oriented, but that doesn't mean that you have to be a model to be attractive. The prettier you feel, the prettier you look. The more comfortable you are with yourself and your body, the more at ease men will be with you. The more open and approachable you are, the more inviting you will be. Try being more flirtatious, just for fun. Start wearing some color in your clothing. Find out which colors better suit you and start wearing them more often. Start wearing clothes that compliment your body type rather than accentuate the things you don't like. Start looking, acting, and feeling like you want to be noticed and approached by a man. You will be *amazed* how many new opportunities will start presenting themselves. Face it. Your family loves you. Your friends love you and accept you for who you are, but you can't expect men to look hard to find your inner beauty. You have to wear it, show it, feel it, and love it. You will feel a whole lot better when you do, regardless of whether a man is in the picture or not.

The Girl-Next-Door Type

Keep in mind that being comfortable with your body and being flirtatious, and even sexy, does not mean having sex with men. The same advice that mothers may have given you ladies when you were adolescents is no less true just because you are mature women now: Men desire the sexy woman, but want to marry the "girl next door." When men are asked what attributes they would like to see in the woman they marry, this is what they often say:

- She should be a good friend, someone he could talk to and who understands him.
- She needs to have the kind of values that would make for a good wife.
- If a man has a son or daughter, even if already an adult, a woman should be a good stepmother to his children.
- They should have things in common.
- She should be open, approachable, and receptive.
- She should help a man feel good about himself.
- She is feminine and sexy, but not "slutty."
- She still likes having sex.
- She is fun to be with.

All right. You can laugh all you want, but guys still want a woman who is a lady in public, makes him look and feel good, and is a lot of fun in private. Men put all these attributes ahead of being "a fox" when it comes down to whom they want to marry.

Dance of Nature

Similar to watching a *National Geographic* special, the interplay between men and women in the dating process is not unlike a dance of nature. The woman needs to assume a feminine posture so that the man will be attracted, yet be very selective in her choice. In nature, it is the *male* who has to exert the most energy so as to be chosen in the courtship dance. Males vie for the female. It is no different in our culture. Certainly there are exceptions, but they are in the minority. Even as women assume greater roles and professional responsibilities, the dance remains the same in the personal sphere. Many women make the mistake of working too hard in the beginning stage of a relationship, as if trying to win the man over. Act like *he* has to work for *you*. Men like that as they are naturally competitive and like a challenge.

Caution! Many (not all) men may initially convey that they are interested in a deeper relationship fairly quickly. He may take measures to become involved faster, calling you often and saying that he wants to see you. Naturally, the topic of sex arises fairly quickly as well. Many women find this level of attention flattering and welcome it. After all, it may have been a while since a man showed this kind of interest. Be forewarned: As quickly as a man can engage, he can disengage. Such is a common complaint of women, particularly after they engage in sex with a man prematurely. If a man really likes you and wants to get to know you, he will wait. It is up to the woman to set the pace in the relationship and to establish limits. Such a posture will only make you more attractive to a man, activating a sense of challenge in him. The generated tension in the male can actually fuel an idealized image about you, an image that men tend to have about women. A smart woman wants to maintain this image, which keeps men in their courtship posture.

Sex and Relationships

Some Women Have Asked: If I Don't Have Sex with a Man after a Few Dates, Won't He Give Up and Go Elsewhere? As I stated in an earlier chapter, if a woman can't afford to say "no" to having sex, she can't afford to say "yes." To have sex out of fear or even intimidation is a horrible way to be in a relationship. Do you really want to be in a relationship with a man who is not able to be patient or control his impulses or who tries to make you feel bad if you set a reasonable limit? If you are not able to reasonably address such a matter at the beginning of a relationship with a man, can you imagine what it will be like later on concerning other things?

Other Women Have Asked: What If I'm the One Who Wants to Have Sex? A woman wanting to have sex with a man she likes and is attracted to makes sense. However, (Pardon the repetition) having sex with a candidate changes the relationship in ways that make it difficult to manage. Once you have sex, if you find that he really isn't your type after all or he concludes similarly, it is more difficult to reestablish a more distant stance without someone feeling hurt or used. Also, when sex becomes a primary focus of the relationship, it tends to overshadow exploring other aspects.

Forget the "Fixer-Upper"

A common complaint is that the older the woman, the fewer good men there are to choose from. As a consequence, some make the mistake of settling for men they think they are going to "fix" while in the relationship. This is a concept that hasn't worked for others in the past, and it won't work any better today. You are much better off making a decision about a man "as is." Either he is good enough the way he is, or leave him alone for both your sakes. Healthy relationships are about how people influence, rather than change and control, one another.

Men Look for a Good Friend in a Woman

Women are more likely to have another woman as a best friend and the one they talk to about sensitive matters. Most men look to their girlfriends and life partners to be their best friends and the ones to whom they talk about sensitive subjects (if they are going to talk about them at all). Equally true is the fact that many men have difficulty feeling emotionally vulnerable, including in a relationship. When a man experiences you as safe, nurturing, and engaging, he is more likely to be drawn to you and self-disclose. While you are having this experience with a man, be mindful to maintain a supportive, understanding posture. When a man discloses and feels vulnerable, he is going to be vigilant for any negativity or criticism from you. If he does not find any, he will sense more of an emotional connection with you and will likely want to be with you again. Asking questions that foster conversation is good, but be sure to look for clues to his reaction. If he looks uncomfortable, gently back off from the topic of conversation and try to make a supportive statement.

Wanda was on her second date with Tyler when the topic of children came up. Tyler became sad, serious, and upset as he told the story of how he became estranged from his grown children, who were in their early to mid-twenties, during the divorce process. Wanda realized that this was a difficult, sensitive subject for Tyler and noted this, giving him the option to stop or continue. Tyler stated he hadn't had an opportunity to talk about it in a long time and missed his son and daughter. Wanda listened, refraining from giving Tyler advice. Instead, she made supportive statements regarding how hard it must be for him.

Wanda may have had an opinion about what Tyler was saying and may even have wonderful advice to give, but their relationship was too new to handle such interchanges. Tyler would most likely feel misunderstood and criticized, even if Wanda was right. What if Wanda made the mistake of taking the conversation too far?

As Tyler expressed bitterness over his ex-wife turning their son and daughter against him for wanting a divorce, Wanda innocently asked Tyler what measures he had taken to contact his adult children. Tyler became defensive and annoyed at her question, telling Wanda that he tried several times to no avail. Wanda picked up on his reaction and apologized for her question. She told him she understood how important children are and how much it wounds when they become rejecting. Children sometimes feel or are made to feel that they have to choose sides. Wanda was trying to help because she saw how much Tyler was in pain. Tyler apologized for his reaction, saying how frustrated he was that his son and daughter still refused to talk to him.

Such an interchange, though uncomfortable, is good information for Wanda. She learned that Tyler could talk about emotionally sensitive subjects, that he acknowledges when he has erred, and that he can recoup his demeanor constructively. At the same time, Wanda realized that Tyler becomes easily defensive and may not be used to reconciling his actions with his emotional experience, a shortcoming on his part. Keeping in mind that everybody has shortcomings, what is important is how Tyler responds to Wanda and her efforts to clarify her intent. She needs to know if he can use her positive efforts constructively. Such an interchange can demonstrate whether a relationship is workable so that mistakes are made but can be resolved. Once again, as unfair as it is, many men tend to look to women to set the pace and be in charge of the emotional tenor of the interchanges between them. You can judge men poorly for this, but if you exclude such men as potential candidates, you will be left with pretty slim pickings. That doesn't mean that a man can't be emotionally understanding or supportive of you.

If He Reveals His True Nature

Conventional wisdom says that some things are so obvious they do not need to be said. However, there are matters that are so important that they must be addressed. If a male candidate reveals his true nature to you, whether positive or negative, believe him. If he is sweet, considerate, thoughtful, and communicative with you, but easily angered, rude, condescending, or even abusive with others, it is just a matter of time before he will be that way with you. If a man is ever violent or threatening, run fast and far, and lose his number even if he sincerely apologizes to you afterwards. This is true even when he offers what sounds like a good, reasonable explanation for his behavior. You can be sure that was not the first time it happened, despite what he might say, and it most certainly will not be the last.

There are men looking for a life partner, as you are. Others pretend they are and are really players. Others, still, are too confused to know what they want but may be open to possibilities. Some may not be.

What Is a Player and How Can You Spot One

A player is a guy who likes to date women but really is not interested in marriage or a long-term relationship. He wants entertainment, companionship, and sex but not commitment. Even if he submits to a monogamous relationship, either he doesn't adhere to it or he only does for a short while. Relationships with a player usually don't last too long. His résumé of relationships with women is very long, and there is always a reason why the relationship didn't last. According to him it is usually because of a woman's shortcoming. Some of the more popular reasons include:

- I haven't found the right woman. *(Of course, you could be the one!)*
- She wanted more than I could give her. *(So don't ask too much of me.)*
- She was a bitch, and I didn't know it at first. *(Don't you feel sorry for me?)*
- Bad luck in relationships. *(You're next.)*
- My first marriage ended in a bitter divorce. *(Even though it was ten-plus years ago.)*

Some of the more benign reasons given are:

- My career is very demanding. *(Relationships are of low*

priority.)
- My kids needed me. *(No room for anybody else.)*
- I was taking care of my sick mother. *(Even though she died years ago.)*

Benign or not, the result is still the same; players are not available. Their reasons just cover up the fact that they really don't want to get married. They may like the idea of marriage, but not what goes along with it. Players can present very well as they have had lots of practice going out with women. They know how to chase and pursue you, but they can vanish like smoke when they get what they want or you want more of a commitment.

Maintaining a Proper Stance

When you maintain the proper stance in your Apprenticeship to Love program, you don't have to worry since you will have the opportunity to find out who is a player and who is not. In fact, you can become an expert in spotting the difference when you take your time to find out. Players tend not to stick around when they don't get what they want in their time frame.

Even with the warning I just gave about certain males, overall, you don't have to be scared or intimidated by men. Some present with bravado, and some with high self-assurance. Others are shy and reserved. In the end, they are human with strengths and vulnerabilities just like you.

Chapter 6 is written for male apprentices in their efforts to be more effective with female candidates. You are welcome to read this chapter, but be forewarned that it is written with men in mind. What is said is a matter of opinion from a male's perspective and not meant to offend women.

Chapter Review:
Just for Women

What you need to know:

- Dispelling the myth that a man is supposed to choose the woman for a relationship is the first step in empowering women in the Apprenticeship to Love program.
- The more experience you have with men, the less intimidated you will surely be as you realize they have their vulnerabilities and insecurities too.
- In the Apprenticeship to Love program, you are being trained to become more comfortable in the presence of men, in engaging them, and in learning about them through experience.
- Guys want a woman who is a lady in public, makes him look and feel good, and is a lot of fun in private. Men put all these attributes ahead of being "a fox" when it comes down to whom they want to marry.
- Many women make the mistake of working too hard in the beginning stage of a relationship, as if trying to win the man over. Act like *he* has to work for *you*. Men like that since they are naturally competitive and like a challenge.
- Be forewarned: As quickly as a man can engage, he can disengage. Such is a common complaint of women, particularly after they engage in sex with a man prematurely.
- If a woman can't afford to say "no" to having sex, she can't afford to say "yes."
- Having sex with a candidate changes the relationship in ways that make it difficult to manage.
- Forget the "fixer-upper." Either the candidate is good

enough the way he is, or leave him alone for both your sakes.

- Many men have difficulty feeling emotionally vulnerable, including in a relationship. When a man discloses and feels vulnerable, he is going to be vigilant for any negativity or criticism from you.
- If a man is ever violent or threatening, run fast and far, and lose his number even if he sincerely apologizes to you afterwards.
- Learn to spot a player. A player is a guy who likes to date women but really is not interested in marriage or a long-term relationship.

Chapter 6
Just For Men

It is not right, it is not fair, yet it is fact. Despite how some men may feel, it is easier for a man to find a new love relationship after divorce or widowhood than it is for a woman. "So how come I can't get a date or find my kind of woman?" you might ask. The main reason is likely to be due to:

1) Shyness or intimidation
2) Looking in the wrong places, or
3) Not knowing or not understanding the basic rules of initiating contact and relating to potential women candidates.

Shyness Factor

Let's first talk about the shyness factor. If you are shy just around women, congratulations; this is the most common and the most treatable form of shyness among single guys. The solution is to have repeated exposure to women in a way that allows you to gain mastery over your reaction.

Whenever Ron thought about approaching a woman socially, he would become so anxious that he avoided almost any opportunity that presented itself. The thought of going to a party or social gathering to meet a potential candidate would make his heart beat "loud" and fast to the point that he thought others could actually hear it. His palms would sweat so much that he kept wiping them, and he was embarrassed at the idea of shaking anybody's hand. Ron's coach, Tim, decided that Ron first had to get used to being comfortable talking and interacting with women before trying to meet one to date. He began by having Ron initiate casual conversation with women he came in contact with, whether he knew the person or not. Tim would have Ron say hello, comment on the weather or any other neutral topic, and see what happened. If a woman responded, Ron would briefly continue the discussion with her until the conversation reached its conclusion, and then he would end with "Have a nice day." If the woman didn't respond or gave him a look of disapproval, Ron was to smile and just look away. Ron tried it while standing in line at the coffee shop, while waiting for a meeting to start, or anywhere he saw the opportunity. He was amazed at how many women responded favorably. They seemed to understand that he was simply being friendly.

Voila! That is the key to successfully meeting women in any new social situation. Just be friendly and make casual conversation, expecting *nothing*. Starting this way makes you and the woman both feel at ease. Once you are engaged in conversation, you have an opportunity to experience how she is responding to you. Look for visual clues. Does she seem to enjoy your company and conversation? If so, simply continue. If not, move on. Nothing ventured, nothing lost. Once you are more comfortable with making the initial contact with women, it is just a matter of expanding the experience in settings that promote longer exchanges, like parties and other social gatherings. Expecting nothing is very liberating as you really aren't taking a risk. All you are looking for is pleasant conversation and nice interchanges. In doing so, you will have a very nice time wherever you are and you will have access to more women than you imagined.

Steven took his Apprenticeship to Love program very seriously. He seemed to run out of places to meet women through his usual resources so he decided to expand his circle. *Not only did he go to his class reunion, but he started asking his friends if he could join them at theirs, as well as any other social functions that sounded interesting. Random introductions and discussions are part and parcel of such settings. He was explaining to Betty, one of the women he met (who was married), his quest to meet other interesting, single women for his networking program. She said Steven had to meet her friend, Rita, who was at the reunion as well.*

Women as Resources

Fact: Women are the best sources of introduction to other women for men. They know single women in their family and social circle who would love to be introduced to a decent guy who is seriously looking for a good relationship (rather than just "a player"). Because women are the gatekeepers of introductions, your time is well spent speaking to them. Remember, you are just being friendly and making conversation, so it doesn't matter if they are single or married. If the woman is married and you two are relating well, you might want to tell her about your networking program to find a life partner and of the strict parameter of no sex with the candidates. The minute you tell a woman about your Apprenticeship to Love program, she is going to look at you in a very different way. Now she is likely to be "checking you out" to see if you really mean it and might ask questions to learn more about you. If she likes you, you just might get an introduction out of the conversation. If not, you haven't lost anything and you still gained experience.

Scary Women

Everybody knows that there *are* some scary people out there that you want to stay away from. However, sometimes men feel nervous or even inadequate when they meet emotionally strong, successful, and/or beautiful women. At times, a man will compare himself in a competitive way with a woman, and if she is viewed as being more successful or too successful (however defined), the man may feel intimidated. The same is true when a woman is regarded as physically attractive. A man can feel insecure, as if the fact that a woman is attractive means that she will cheat on him. Once a man enters this realm of thinking, he is no longer responding to the actual woman but rather his own fears and insecurities. If you find yourself feeling uncertain, take the time to examine your feelings. You may actually discover that you are not giving yourself (or the woman) credit.

Women apprentices are often much better at the nuances of relationships than men for the same reason that males are unlikely to read the chapter "Just for Women" and females are guaranteed to read this chapter. Men tend to look at life in what they think of as more "practical" terms, simplifying matters. They can't understand why women complicate things. Women like to talk, understand, and "work through." Men like to fix, move on, and forget about it. Thus the great divide between the sexes. Here are some guidelines that can be like a survivor's guide in your dealings with women.

A Survivor's Guide for Men about Women

Understanding Women

Forget thinking that you are going to ultimately understand women. A man can get very confused trying to do so. With women, it can feel like the rules always seem to be changing. The fact is that women think differently than men. They like to "process." They like to communicate by trying to figure out what happened and why it happened. That's a woman's way of relating and feeling intimate. Don't fight it as it only makes you look bad. Besides, a lot of the time, it's actually a good thing.

Paul had been dating Mary for several weeks. He began to arrive late, especially when he was coming from visiting his teenaged daughters at his ex-wife's house. Paul was always very apologetic about his tardiness, saying how uncharacteristic it was for him to be late, which made Mary even more curious. After Paul arrived late, yet again, she asked for details about what had detained him. Paul became annoyed at the question, though he couldn't explain why. After all, Mary was asking a reasonable question. He figured it might be because he had always been protective of his daughters and didn't like answering questions about them. As the details unfolded about this and recent other times when he was late, Paul realized that after he had told his daughters about Mary, they began to ask him for help each time he got ready to leave them to meet Mary. He began to consider that maybe his daughters were reacting to the news of this new woman in his life.

Initiating First Contact

Most women wait for the man to initiate contact. You need to look for "the signal" from her that she is interested in being approached by you. Look carefully because it is usually subtle. For example, she can repeatedly glance at you, following your movements as you walk around the room. She may place herself in your line of sight or move to a location that would make it easier for you to meet her. It is a kind of choreographed dance of nature that you need to pick up on in order to understand. Many men hate initiating contact, afraid that they are reading the signal wrong and will be embarrassed.

Larry was at a party when he spotted Sandy, whom he thought would be interesting to meet. He casually walked over to an area of the room where it would be easier for her to notice him, which she did. Sandy gave him a quick glance and smiled slightly. She was talking to another person but positioned herself so that she could see Larry better. She looked at him from time to time, letting Larry know that she was at least curious. Not long after that, Sandy made her move by going toward the beverage area not far from where Larry had been standing. Larry made sure he got there first and asked Sandy if he could get her something. She asked for a glass of water, and they began to make casual conversation about the party. The conversation ended quickly, and Sandy did not seem responsive to Larry's efforts to engage her in another subject. Larry excused himself, stating the need to get back to the friend he had been talking to, and told her to enjoy the rest of the party.

The interchange did not work out, but nothing bad happened here. It was a friendly exchange that involved very little risk. Larry did not have to be embarrassed because there were no expectations.

Pursuing Unavailable Women

Do not pursue a woman who does not want to be with you. Just move on to the next potential candidate. Challenges can be fun, but this program is not about conquests. Once you initiate contact, a woman will often make efforts to maintain a dialogue with you when she is interested. It is her way of letting you know that she is happy to be in your presence and wants to keep the interchange going between you. If she keeps looking away or acts as if she is bored, bothered, or not interested, simply find any plausible excuse to move away from her like Larry did with Sandy.

Sandy said that she, too, had to get back to her friends but invited Larry to come and meet them, which he did.

Larry had erred on the side of caution. Sandy realized that she had given him the wrong signal and corrected it with the invitation. As you can see, it is an unfolding process that gives you information that helps you gauge your actions.

Talking to Women

Women like to converse and interact in a social setting. Talk to the woman you have met about what you like to do for fun or sport. Tell her what activities you are involved in. When you do, she is likely to feel as if she would be better getting to know you. Ask what interests her and what she likes to do and then listen, looking at her and paying attention. She is likely to view you as taking an interest in her as a person, which is very favorable when in the presence of a woman.

Warning: If you stop talking to a woman, become unresponsive, or become distracted (e.g., by the ball game on the TV), she is likely to think you a boor or she will feel you dislike her, both of which will work against you if you really are interested in her.

Dennis met Joy at a holiday party. The conversation between them was going well when Dennis seemed to run out of things to say. He really enjoyed Joy's company but didn't know what to talk about or do next. Dennis apologized, saying that he was not used to talking so much, which was reassuring to Joy. She understood that Dennis was just stuck in a lull in their conversation so she asked him about what she had just learned was his favorite sport, baseball, which gave Dennis much more to talk about.

For Dennis, being direct about what was happening was useful. Once Joy understood what the problem was, she could do something to help.

Let a Woman Get to Know You

Women equate intimacy with the sharing of thoughts and feelings. Disclosing your thoughts and feelings on subjects being discussed is likely to be experienced as positive by a woman. She will see this as you being emotionally available, which is highly valued. Be careful not to over-disclose about the trials and tribulations of your past, particularly in the first couple of meetings. Let her first see and experience your strengths and how much fun you can be. Besides, women often like a little bit of mystery about the man they are talking to. It makes them want to know more about you. Remember to ask about her thoughts and feelings. It will help you get to know her, and this will tell her that you care enough to ask.

A Woman's Eyes Are in Her Head

Look a woman in the eyes when talking to her. Avoid talking to her chest as there are no eyes or ears there.

Be a Gentleman

Act like a gentleman. Show a woman that chivalry is not dead. Open her door. Take an interest in her comfort. Women have a high regard for thoughtfulness and being considered. They feel cared about and special. Besides, isn't that how you want to feel about the woman you are dating?

Keep the Interaction Nonsexual

Don't get sexually physical with candidates. Relating to women in nonphysical or nonsexual ways keeps the interaction between you easy, relaxed, and without unnecessary pressures. It preserves a more manageable relationship. Remember that maintaining safety, regard, and respect for your women candidates is paramount in the Apprenticeship to Love program. Candidates are meant to be replaced, and you do not want to leave a trail of women feeling hurt and used in the process. You want to enjoy a woman's company and discover her many other sides. Your self-restraint lets her know that you are interested in her as a person, not a sex object. You don't have to pretend that there isn't sexual energy between you. In fact, it can be reassuring, fun, and flattering. Just redirect it to other areas of relating.

Kevin met Beverly on an Internet dating service and had several e-mail contacts and a couple of telephone conversations with her before setting up a face-to-face meeting. Some of their interchanges had even gotten a little risqué, piquing Kevin's interest. He certainly was not disappointed when he met Beverly, who was very attractive. Physical chemistry between them was evident from the start. Realizing this, Kevin took special care to stay in public places when he got together with Beverly. As he spent more time with her, Kevin realized just how different he and Beverly were. Aside from the physical attraction and a shared passion for music, they were too different in many fundamental ways. He spoke to Beverly about it, and they agreed to continue a friendship based on their love of music, occasionally going to concerts together.

Kevin and Beverly were able to shift their relationship because it had remained within manageable emotional parameters. The relationship was guided by social and interpersonal aspects, not by hormones. Even if Beverly did not feel good about Kevin's observations, she could see that he was right. She did not feel used or taken advantage of, which is how many women feel after men end a relationship subsequent to having sex with them.

Respect "No" from Women

No means no. Respect the limits that a woman sets. It is not entertaining or endearing for a woman to have a man disregard her efforts to set a limit. A woman regards this to be abusive, and it is!

Pay for the Date

Don't be cheap when going out with a woman; pick up the tab. If you are on a tight budget, look for places with a view or atmosphere rather than those that are expensive. Women consider atmosphere romantic.

Roger was working hard on his Apprenticeship to Love program, meeting and going out with as many women as he could in his search for candidates. Being a salaried employee and paying for child support, he could not afford to take all the women he met to restaurants to talk. Instead, he tried to have the initial meetings during the day, choosing a coffee shop facing a park, a pond, or anything scenic that would create a nice atmosphere. If an evening meeting was planned, Roger would try to do it during the week when most people's time is limited and a short get-together is the norm.

Be Decisive

Women like men who are decisive. They consider the male taking the initiative in setting plans as the correct dating posture. When planning to meet with a woman, have suggestions ready for where to go, what to do, and where to meet. Ask, don't assume, and have a back-up plan. If she doesn't favor your suggestions, ask her what she likes to do and choose from her ideas. If the two of you can't come up with a single common activity after discussing each other's interests and involvements, the likelihood is that you probably have very little in common. It may simply not be a good fit between you. Lose the number and look for someone else to meet.

Never Give Up

Don't give up. Remember that there are women out there who want to meet you and be in a relationship. To paraphrase an old saying, "Every jar has a lid that fits. It's just that sometimes you have to keep looking till you find it." If you are not meeting new women or women who are your type, maybe you have exhausted your social circle and it is time to break into a new one.

What Women Want

So, what do women *really* want from male suitors? They want to be prized, appreciated, regarded, respected, validated, pursued, and romanced. Sound impossible? It is a lot easier than you might think. If you treat and relate to a woman as if she's an attractive and desirable person, enjoy her company by listening and responding to what she says, and look for ways to have fun with her, there is a good chance that both of you will feel good about it. After all, if you like the woman you are with, it is not hard to do.

Let us say that you have met and are having a relationship with the woman you want to spend the rest of your life with. What is it that you have to know to keep the love alive between the two of you? Chapter 7 will help you have what everybody wants and few attain: a love relationship that lasts.

Chapter Review:
Just for Men

Did you know?

- It is easier for a mature man to find a new love relationship after divorce or widowhood than it is for a woman.
- The solution to shyness around women is to have repeated exposure to them in a way that allows you to gain mastery over your reaction.
- Women are the best sources of introduction to other women.

A survivor's guide on women

- Women think differently than men. They like to "process." They like to communicate by trying to figure out what happened and why it happened. That's a woman's way of relating and feeling intimate.
- Most women wait for the man to initiate contact. You need to look for "the signal" from her that she is interested in being approached by you.
- Do not pursue a woman who does not want to be with you.
- Women like to converse and interact in a social setting. Talk to the woman you have met about what you like to do for fun or sport. Ask what interests her and what she likes to do and then listen, looking at her and paying attention.
- If you stop talking to a woman, become unresponsive, or become distracted (e.g., by the ball game on the TV), she is likely to think you a boor or she will feel you dislike her.
- Women equate intimacy with the sharing of thoughts

and feelings. Disclosing your thoughts and feelings on subjects being discussed is likely to be experienced as positive by a woman.

- Look a woman in the eyes when talking to her. Avoid talking to her chest as there are no eyes or ears there.
- Act like a gentleman. Show a woman that chivalry is not dead.
- Don't get sexually physical with candidates. Relating to women in nonphysical or nonsexual ways keeps the interaction between you easy, relaxed, and without unnecessary pressures.
- No means no. Respect the limits that a woman sets.
- Don't be cheap when going out with a woman; pick up the tab. If you are on a tight budget, look for places with a view or atmosphere rather than those that are expensive.
- Women like men who are decisive. They consider the male taking the initiative in setting plans as the correct dating posture.

Chapter 7
From Apprentice to Marital Partner

Apprenticeship After Marriage

While your search for a life partner ends after marriage, your apprenticeship does not. The process of learning continues as you understand more about yourself, your love partner, and the life that you have together. If you stop investing in yourself and your love partner, your relationship *will* become stale and boring (and so will you). Consequently, you will start taking each other for granted.

How to Safeguard a Healthy Marital Relationship

Keeping a marriage healthy and viable requires work. Both partners must maintain a commitment to:

- The three Cs of a successful relationship: Caring, Communication, and Commitment
- Saying "I'm sorry" and meaning it
- Keeping passion and fun in the relationship
- Perpetual personal growth

The Three Cs: Caring, Communication, Commitment

Caring, communication, and commitment are fundamental building blocks in any successful, long-term relationship. *Caring* is the first and most familiar in people's minds. It involves liking the other person, feeling good about him or her, having an emotional attachment to that person, experiencing a sense of love, wanting to be in that person's presence, and having an affinity toward that person. Caring brings a smile to your face when you see or think about your mate. Ironically, this warm and fuzzy feeling that is central to a relationship, also known as intimacy, naturally diminishes in the experience of a couple over the course of time.[4] Unfortunately, it diminishes even faster if the couple lives with children in the household.[5] This does not mean that it disappears or is less important to each person, but it does mean that the feeling becomes more distant in the couple's awareness. Each person loses some of the sense of closeness that used to be so central in the earlier part of the relationship. In some cases, it is due to neglect; in others, taking the relationship for granted; and in many cases, distractions made by life's demands. Some may become so distant from it that they question the entire relationship. The good news is that the caring may have simply gone underground and just needs to be exposed.

Bruce and Kathleen, both in their late fifties, had been married for ten years in a second union for both. Bruce, having leftover bills from his first marriage, had to work many hours in his business to catch up financially. Somewhere in those early years, Bruce and Kathleen both felt a distance grow between them. Bruce wrote this off as normal due to stress and the many hours spent apart. Several years later, Bruce found himself feeling lonely and increasingly isolated in the marriage. Traveling on business trips did not seem to help, and he began to have an increased awareness of other women he was meeting. Then, Kathleen had a health scare when her doctor found a lump in her breast. Bruce refocused his attention

---

4   Robert J. Sternberg, *Cupid's Arrow: The Course of Love through Time* (Cambridge, United Kingdom: Cambridge University Press, 1998).
5   Lawrence A. Kurdeck, "The Nature and Predictors of the Trajectory of Change in Marital Quality for Husbands and Wives over the First 10 Years of Marriage," *Developmental Psychology* Vol. 35, 5 (1999): 1283–1296.

on Kathleen, making more time to be with her, talking to her more, even while away, and letting her know that he was there for her. Though the lump turned out to be benign, the ordeal brought Bruce and Kathleen closer together. Bruce was surprised how close he felt to Kathleen again and realized he had been distracted from the marriage. He vowed to reinvest in and refocus on the relationship, realizing that he could have lost both Kathleen and the marriage.

Kathleen's health scare blew away the shroud of complacency and the routine of everyday life, revealing a deeper connection in the relationship. It is not hard to lose focus on a relationship in the hectic, demanding life that most people live, and it is very easy to take things for granted. Even good feelings that we do not want to lose can fall prey to inadvertent neglect, becoming buried over time. Making conscious efforts and engaging in behaviors that remind us of how important our spouse is help us maintain that sense of closeness. For example, by going out on dates with each other and being involved in activities that are fun, you are reminded of what brought you two together in the first place. Most important, by developing and maintaining the next "C," *communication*, you maintain emotional access to one another.

Communication is the lifeline of any relationship. It is more than simply talking to each other. In fact, effective communication begins with active, productive listening. You can only effectively respond to what you first fully understand. Communication involves expressing thoughts, feelings, concerns, dreams, and basically anything deemed relevant to oneself and the relationship. It lets you be known and understood by your spouse and vice versa. It allows each spouse to become aware of and suggest creative ideas for keeping the relationship fun and interesting as well as for addressing matters that can potentially get in the way. The more honest and straightforward you are with one another, the better. You should understand that the more you do not want to talk with your spouse about something that has the potential to weaken the relationship, *the more you have to!* The relationship becomes stronger and more powerful when you have the means and access to address anything that has the potential to harm your relationship.

Her children grown and no longer living with her, Cheryl went back to work at a job in sales that she liked and that challenged her intellectually. Because of her visibility, she decided to lose weight and dress more fashionably. The better she looked, the better she felt about herself, drawing increased attention from men she met. Cheryl tried to increase the spark between herself and Wayne, her husband, but he didn't seem to be paying attention. The more frustrated Cheryl became, the more responsive she was to other men's attention and nearly had an affair. She confronted Wayne about what she perceived to be his lukewarm interest in her and called his attention to the fact that other men seemed to be interested. She confided that, while she had not had an affair, she found herself noticing other men more. She added that she did not want to be with another man but wanted Wayne to take greater interest in her. Wayne was startled by Cheryl's disclosure. He initially felt hurt, threatened, and betrayed by Cheryl's revelation but then realized that she had done nothing wrong. In fact, Cheryl was trying to save the marriage. Wayne simply didn't like what Cheryl was saying, and he was being defensive.

Caution: Being able to constructively say what has been a source of worry and concern often unburdens the person who has these feelings. However, some revelations may need to be made in a setting such as a counselor's office when there is uncertainty whether the other person knows how to deal with such disclosures in a healthy fashion.

Cheryl can be considered courageous for her revelation to Wayne, though some of you may question her wisdom. When spouses constructively and successfully address an issue that both realize could have impeded or destroyed the relationship, the marriage is affirmed and the couple is brought closer together. Just as a chain is only as strong as its weakest link, a marriage is only as strong as the couple's ability to resolve differences and tensions constructively. Effective communication is the means towards that end. It is also the means of introducing new ideas that keep the relationship interesting and vibrant.

Cheryl and Wayne considered what they could do for fun and to reinvest in the relationship. Cheryl always wanted to be able to dance with Wayne at parties, but he did not like to because he didn't know how. Wayne always wanted to share his love for fly-fishing with Cheryl, but she was never interested. Wayne agreed to take ballroom dance classes, and Cheryl agreed to take fly-fishing classes and go on two fishing excursions with Wayne.

Each realized the emotional investment and time commitment by the other and felt heard, considered, and loved. The make-up sex was great.

The third "C," *commitment*, is the promise couples make when they marry to stay with one another. It is the dedication to make the relationship work no matter what life may throw their way. Commitment is the glue that keeps couples together and gives them the opportunity to work things out when one or both feel like quitting.

Patrick and Theresa were having a hard time with one another. Each had his or her own set of complaints and a list of wrongdoings by the other. Patrick and Theresa both realized they had hit bottom in their relationship and were in trouble. They had been together for close to thirty years, which was not too long to be able to recall all the good and bad they had faced together. They also had two adult children, a loving extended family, a close circle of friends, a comfortable lifestyle each liked, and the memory of how things had been when they enjoyed each other. Neither wanted to give up all the good that accompanied their marital relationship. Patrick and Theresa spoke for a very long time. They agreed to seek out a marital counselor to help them.

Because leaving the relationship is not an option in a committed union, other choices tend to be considered. However, commitment alone does not make for a good long-term relationship. You also need the combination of a maintained sense of caring and good communication in order to have the recipe for a successful relationship.

The Power of Apology

As I stated in an earlier chapter, a healthy, happy long-term relationship requires its partners to be able to sincerely say, "I am sorry." It does not have to come easily as long as it happens. When said appropriately and with sincerity, this short but powerful phrase can disarm an angry or hurt spouse and begin the process of bridging the gap between a couple in conflict.

When a love partner feels hurt or angry, the tendency is to create distance or to emotionally disconnect from the person perceived to have caused the pain. When at least one of the members is not considering the thoughts and feelings of the other, the process of trying to reconcile differences becomes difficult if not impossible. Saying "I'm sorry" conveys to the other person:

- I am considering your thoughts, feelings, and point of view.
- I have regard for you.
- I don't like being at odds with you.
- There is something that I have said or done that has hurt you, even if unintentional.
- I am trying to do something constructive.

Apologizing does not mean you are taking responsibility for an entire problem. It is an acknowledgement that there may have been something you said, did, or did not do that has caused pain or distress to the other person (intentionally or unintentionally). Most conflict in relationships is based on misunderstanding that can be readily resolved when both partners are prepared to do so.

Fred came home to Fran giving him the cold shoulder and silent treatment. He asked what was wrong, and she reminded him that he said he was coming home for dinner at 6:00 PM and it was now 9:00 PM. She and the children waited for him for over an hour before eating. Fred never called to let her know he would be late. Now Fred was angry. He was tired, hungry, and feeling unappreciated. Fred had come from an important but unscheduled business meeting, and he felt unable to take a break to call Fran. Fran expressed her appreciation for his work, adding that she was worried about him. All she wanted was a call or text message. Fred apologized, saying he would have appeared "weak" at the meeting if he had stopped to call Fran but could have sent her a quick text message.

Successful long-term relationships are based on the premise that it is more important to be "happy" than "right."

Passion: Keeping the Excitement in the Relationship

It is not surprising that research shows that passion wanes over the course of a long-term relationship,[6] yet passion remains an important ingredient of a healthy, intimate marriage. While passion in a love relationship is often thought of as the act of having sex, it is actually much more complex in a marriage, and it reflects intertwined physical and emotional needs. Passion in marriage is associated with feeling vibrant, alive, deeply in

---

6   Sternberg, *Cupid's Arrow.*

love, safe, attractive, sexually satisfied, taken care of, dominant or submissive, powerful, and much more. A lack of passion in marriage can engender feeling bored, unhappy, unloved, unattractive, inadequate, frustrated, and empty. The dilemma in marriage is the need for passion, yet passion is known to naturally wane over time.

Why Passion Lessens Over Time

Ironically, a sense of contentment and self-satisfaction can lead spouses to conclude, "If it ain't broke, don't fix it," striving to keep things the same. Life becomes dictated by set routines for the sake of efficiency. This can lead to taking many things for granted, including each other. If there are no interchanges between spouses that excite the senses, one or both can begin to feel bored, unchallenged, and unfulfilled. Make-up sex can be wonderful. Why? Because what preceded it created an imbalance in the relationship, reminding marital partners not to take things for granted. There is heightened emotionality between the spouses and maybe even nervousness as to whether the relationship will be okay. The sex after reconciliation acts as a release of tension and an affirmation of the relationship.

Scott forgot Judith's birthday. She was hurt, angry, and felt taken for granted. Scott knew he "dropped the ball" and repeatedly apologized to his wife. He reminded Judith of the recent pressures at work and the extra hours he had been working. Judith said that she had been supportive and understanding of him, but that didn't excuse his forgetting about her. Scott bought tickets to a show he knew Judith wanted to see and made reservations at her favorite restaurant before the theater. Scott told Judith how much he loved her and how important she was to him, taking full responsibility for the oversight. Judith knew Scott's mistake was unintentional and saw that he was trying to make it up to her. They made passionate love. Scott and Judith felt closer, comforted, and understood.

Scott's forgetfulness disrupted how things usually were in the marital relationship. The situation raised questions and strong emotions for both. In order to resolve the tension between them, which neither felt good about, each had to consider not only their own feelings, but those of the other spouse, requiring empathy and understanding. This process allowed them to get closer again. The sex became a kind of declaration that all was well between them.

Gregg and Carolyn, both in their late fifties, had been married for twenty-five years. They have a happy, busy, active life together. The problem is that their sex life has diminished tremendously. Carolyn rarely has desire, and when she does, she thinks about how dry and sensitive she has become vaginally as a result of menopause, causing sex to be painful and unappealing. While Gregg does not have a high sex drive, making love to Carolyn is still important to him. Gregg spoke to Carolyn about his frustration, of missing her physically, and of feeling increasingly distant from her. Carolyn was sympathetic, but said she didn't want to be in pain to satisfy him sexually. Both agreed things could not stay the same. Gregg suggested that they try to find ways to please each other that were not painful to her. Together, they planned a relaxed, romantic evening, setting the stage for gentle exploration of pleasurable sensations that satisfy. The experience was intensified by the total concentration they gave one another as each watched for signs of pleasure or discomfort. Afterward, Gregg and Carolyn felt pleased, relaxed, and closer together than they had in a long time.

This second example is a reminder that tension and distance in relationships can be brought about not only through conflict, but by life situations that are nobody's fault. Gregg's expressed sexual frustration signaled an unmet need. Carolyn's concerns being tended to in a supportive way showed caring and attentiveness. Both experienced a sense of risk in bringing up a problem and in taking measures to address it. In the end, both felt considered, understood, and tended to both physically and mentally. No wonder each felt impassioned and pleased!

Couples do not need to fight or have conflict in order to keep passion in the relationship, though some couples seem to do just that. A better strategy would be to engage in activities and behaviors that keep changing the routine in the marriage. Couples need to seek out new ways of having fun together, developing different pursuits and interests individually and as a couple, and exploring new pleasurable experiences together, both in and out of the bedroom. Basically, if you do not seek out and explore new excitement with each other, you are likely to lose the passion between you!

Dan and Gail are having the time of their life. Ever since their son and daughter went off to college, they have been rediscovering what it means to work hard and have fun. Dan and Gail have two kids to put through college, but they also have a new-found freedom they have not had in years. Time is theirs, and they are making the most of it. Dan has become more serious about his golf game, and Gail is taking courses online to finish a degree she had put aside when she had children. They have more time to get together with friends on the weekend, go out on dates together, and talk to each other; both are supportive of one another's pursuits. Dan and Gail find each other more interesting and are exploring new ways to please each other wherever and whenever they want to in their house.

Perpetual Personal Growth: Questions And Answers

Marriage is only as strong and healthy as the weaker, less healthy member. On the other hand, a marriage is made healthier and stronger when both spouses dedicate themselves to becoming better marital partners and better people.

Does one have to become a spiritual guru to be happily married? On the contrary, you would fare better understanding and using the imperfection of the human condition as a working premise. That means *everybody*! If people took the time to listen, consider, and try to understand another person's perspective, rather than simply judging or reacting, we would have a better world and better marriages. This kind of effort is easier said than done in marriage (and life). It requires self-discipline, an unassuming approach, and trust between you and your spouse. You must allow for accountability (by self and spouse), put health and happiness as a high priority, and value positive efforts made by both yourself and your spouse.

Isn't that pretty guruish? Maybe, but what is more important is the dedication of effort. If you want a happy, loving, exciting marriage filled with perpetual intimacy and passion, you have to work hard and consistently for it for the rest of your life. You need to be responsible for yourself, your efforts, and your happiness.

What if only one person in the relationship feels the dedication? You can only do and be what you're capable of. If you have chosen a person committed to being an apprentice of love along with you, it will be a good life together. Learning what it means to have a healthy, evolving love is a lifetime project requiring the participation of both spouses. You want the type of relationship that gives you greater depth of personal meaning and understanding than either one of you can achieve alone. There is nothing better than a love that inspires you to want to be more because you realize that you can be.

How does loving your spouse do that? Through mutual interest and concern in the marriage and devotion to self-improvement. Everybody knows how great a personal accomplishment feels. For example, maybe you have thoughts of pursuing a promotion, going back to school, taking up a new sport, developing a new hobby, or doing anything new or different for yourself that is constructive. Now imagine knowing that your spouse supports your efforts, encourages you, takes an interest in what you are doing, and does what he or she can to help. You would feel pretty grateful, wouldn't you? Now imagine you doing the same thing for your spouse. You can see that your spouse would feel mighty good toward you. What if you did this with each other for the rest of your lives and were able to use your differences as strengths and resources? Can you see what an enriched life that would be? Through exposure and involvement in your life partner's pursuits, you would have experiences that you otherwise would not have. By consciously striving to live a life of love and happiness, you can become aware of personal shortcomings that get in the way for you and your partner; your newfound awareness then becomes the basis of efforts to improve. The result is a lifetime of personal, emotional, and relational growth and meaning. Not a bad life!

Diane had slowly gained weight over the years and was unhappy about it. She wanted to shed the extra weight but struggled in her efforts. She told her husband, Willie, how unhappy she was about it, and he asked what he could do to help. Diane said she wanted to start cooking more vegetable dishes for dinner but didn't want to make a separate meal for him (he's a meat-and-potato kind of guy) since she would end up eating his food too. Knowing how unhappy Diane was, Willie agreed. He encouraged Diane's interest in learning to cook vegetarian cuisine and offered to go for walks with her at night. They began to walk around the neighborhood then switched to going to the boardwalk by the beach. After a while, they looked for easy local hikes with pretty scenery. As time went on, they both became more physically active and joined a hiking club. Diane never knew that losing weight could be so easy. She knew Willie was an important part of her success and was grateful. Willie's cholesterol levels dropped so much as a result of his new diet and exercise that his doctor reduced the dosage of cholesterol medication Willie was taking.

During one of their walks, Willie mentioned to Diane that a promotional exam was being scheduled at his job. Because the test was rarely given, there would certainly be many coworkers taking the test. Willie, a shy and unassuming man, wanted to take the exam, but wondered if he should bother. Diane encouraged Willie to apply for the test, reminding him that he was a respected employee with seniority and was working beyond his job title. Willie knew he could do the job because he had many of the responsibilities of it already. Diane told Willie that she couldn't think of anybody more competent or deserving of the promotion at his job. Willie decided to apply for the promotion and began to prepare for the test. He knew Diane had faith in his abilities, and he wanted to do well for himself and her.

You can see how Diane and Willie influence each other in positive ways and encourage one another. Both are the better for being together.

Does that mean that you can't be fulfilled, truly happy, or be in a life journey of personal growth without finding a good marital partner? You certainly can, by surrounding yourself with loving friendships, but it is difficult for these relationships to reach the depth of impact and meaning that the type of marital union described in this chapter can.

Do you mean to say that if I find the right person to live with and love, I will be happy every day? As you know, life is complicated and challenging. It is filled with details and routines that can feel tedious. Unexpected events can be stressful, frightening, and painful. We are surrounded by a world that can be cruel and unpredictable. Yet here we are, daring to exist. Our happiness and significance depends on what we make of what life sends our way. Being a lifelong apprentice of love means consciously choosing to strive for a life filled with meaning and joy and sharing that journey with a life partner. While it is unlikely that anybody can be happy every day with all of life's challenges, we can certainly strive to be.

Chapter Review:
From Apprentice to Marital Partner

- While your search for a life partner ends after marriage, your apprenticeship does not.
- If you stop investing in yourself and your love partner, your relationship *will* become stale and boring.
- Remember the three Cs of a successful relationship: Caring, Communication, and Commitment.
- Remember to say "I'm sorry" and mean it.
- Strive to keep passion and fun in the relationship.
- Be committed to perpetual personal growth in yourself and in your marital partner.
- Accept being a lifelong apprentice of love, which means consciously choosing to strive for a life filled with meaning and joy and sharing that journey with a life partner.

·

Printed in the United States
219892BV00001B/33/P

9 781440 127687